Super Easy Gas Griddle Cookbook

2000 Days of Delicious & Quick Gas Griddle Recipes for Beginners, Families, and Friends Featuring a 30-Day Meal Plan — Enjoy Summertime and Year-Round Outdoor Meals

Enjoy Nutritious Meals with Unmatched Flavor

Barry Vesper

Legal & Disclaimer

The content and information contained in this book has been compiled from reliable sources, which are accurate based on the knowledge, belief, expertise and information of the Author. The author cannot be held liable for any omissions and/or errors.

TABLE OF CONTENTS

46

INTRODUCTION

Dear readers,

Barry Vesper, a distinguished chef and connoisseur of outdoor cooking, brings his expertise to the world of gas griddle cuisine. This book is your gateway to enjoying both summertime and year-round outdoor feasts.

Gas griddle cooking offers a unique blend of convenience, versatility, and health benefits. The flat, even surface ensures consistent heat distribution, making it perfect for cooking everything from juicy burgers and steaks to delicate fish and crisp vegetables. Cooking on a gas griddle allows you to use less oil, resulting in healthier meals without compromising on flavor. The griddle's ability to handle a variety of foods simultaneously makes it an ideal choice for family meals and entertaining friends.

Barry's recipes are a symphony of flavors, colors, and textures, meticulously crafted to provide quick, nutritious, and delicious meals. His dedication to making outdoor cooking accessible and enjoyable shines through in every recipe. Barry has included a 30-day meal plan to help you get started, making it easy to plan and prepare balanced meals that your whole family will love. The meal plan features a diverse range of dishes rich in proteins, healthy fats, and carbohydrates, ensuring you maintain a healthy diet without sacrificing the joy of eating delicious food.

With Barry Vesper as your guide, your journey into gas griddle cooking will be both manageable and enjoyable. His expertise and enthusiasm will inspire you to create mouth-watering meals, turning every outdoor gathering into a culinary adventure. Embrace the endless possibilities of griddle cooking and enjoy the rich flavors and health benefits it brings. Happy griddling!

CHAPTER 1: GAS GRIDDLE BASICS

Welcome to the World of Gas Griddle Cooking

Whether you're a seasoned chef or just starting your culinary journey, this book is your gateway to mastering the art of gas griddle cooking.

Why Choose Gas Griddle Cooking?

Gas griddle cooking has become a favorite among culinary enthusiasts for several reasons:

Versatility: From breakfast pancakes to juicy burgers, and from delicate fish fillets to hearty steaks, a gas griddle allows you to cook a wide variety of dishes effortlessly.

Efficiency: With even heat distribution and quick temperature adjustments, gas griddles ensure your food is cooked perfectly every time.

Healthier Cooking: Enjoy meals with less oil and fat, as the flat surface of the griddle allows excess grease to drain away from the food.

Outdoor Enjoyment: Whether it's a sunny summer day or a crisp winter evening, cooking on a gas griddle lets you enjoy the great outdoors while preparing delicious meals for your family and friends.

Before diving into the recipes, let's cover some basics to help you make the most of your gas griddle:

Benefits of Using a Gas Griddle

Gas griddles have revolutionized outdoor cooking, offering a blend of convenience, versatility, and superior cooking performance. If you've ever wondered why gas griddles are becoming a staple in backyards across America and the UK, read on to discover the myriad benefits they bring to your culinary experience.

Versatility in Cooking

One of the standout benefits of a gas griddle is its versatility. Unlike traditional grills, which are primarily designed for grilling, gas griddles open up a world of culinary possibilities. Here's what you can do with a gas griddle:

Breakfast Feasts: Cook a full breakfast spread including pancakes, eggs, bacon, and hash browns all at once.

Lunch Delights: Prepare delicious sandwiches, burgers, quesadillas, and more.

Dinner Extravaganza: Grill steaks, seafood, vegetables, and even pizza.

Snacks and Sides: Sauté mushrooms, stir-fry vegetables, or grill some fruit for a tasty dessert.

Even Heat Distribution

Gas griddles are designed to distribute heat evenly across the cooking surface. This ensures that your food cooks uniformly, preventing hotspots and undercooked areas. Whether you're cooking delicate fish fillets or thick steaks, even heat distribution guarantees perfect results every time.

Quick and Efficient Cooking

Gas griddles heat up quickly, allowing you to start cooking in minutes. The efficient heating system not only saves time but also retains heat consistently, making it ideal for both quick meals and elaborate dishes. Say goodbye to long wait times and hello to more time enjoying your meal with family and friends.

Healthier Cooking

Cooking on a gas griddle can be a healthier option compared to traditional frying. Here's why:

Less Oil Needed: The flat surface of the griddle allows you to cook with minimal oil, reducing the fat content of your meals.

Grease Drainage: Most gas griddles come with a built-in grease management system that channels excess grease away from the food, making your meals less greasy and more health-conscious.

Retain Nutrients: Quick and even cooking helps retain the nutrients in your food, ensuring that your meals are not only delicious but also nutritious.

Easy Cleanup

Cleaning up after cooking can be a hassle, but gas griddles simplify this process:

Smooth Surface: The smooth, flat cooking surface is easy to clean. Simply scrape off any food residues and wipe down with a cloth.

Grease Management: The grease tray or cup collects excess grease, making it easy to dispose of without creating a mess.

Durable Materials: Many gas griddles are made from durable materials like stainless steel, which are resistant to stains and rust, ensuring your griddle stays in top condition for years.

Outdoor Cooking Enjoyment

Gas griddles are perfect for outdoor cooking, offering a great way to enjoy the outdoors while preparing delicious meals. Here are a few reasons why:

Social Cooking: Gather around the griddle with family and friends, making cooking a social and interactive experience.

All-Season Cooking: Whether it's a sunny summer day or a chilly winter evening, gas griddles allow you to cook outside all year round.

Space-Saving: Gas griddles are often compact and portable, making them ideal for patios, balconies, and even camping trips.

Cost-Effective

Investing in a gas griddle can be cost-effective in the long run. Here's how:

Energy Efficient: Gas griddles are typically more energy-efficient than traditional grills and ovens, reducing your fuel costs.

Multi-Functional: With the ability to cook a wide variety of meals, a gas griddle eliminates the need for multiple cooking appliances.

Durability: High-quality gas griddles are built to last, offering years of reliable use with minimal maintenance.

Conclusion

The benefits of using a gas griddle are clear: versatility, even cooking, efficiency, healthier meals, easy cleanup, outdoor enjoyment, and cost-effectiveness.

Essential Tools and Equipment

To truly master the art of gas griddle cooking, having the right tools and equipment is crucial. Just as a carpenter is only as good as his tools, a chef's success on the griddle is greatly enhanced by having the right gear. Here's a comprehensive guide to the essential tools and equipment you'll need to elevate your gas griddle cooking experience.

Must-Have Tools

Spatula Set

Wide Spatula: Perfect for flipping burgers, pancakes, and large cuts of meat. The wide surface ensures that your food stays intact during the flip.
Long Spatula: Ideal for handling delicate items like fish fillets and omelets. The length provides better control and precision.
Scraper/Chopper: Useful for cleaning the griddle surface and chopping ingredients directly on the griddle.

Tongs
A good pair of tongs is indispensable for turning sausages, vegetables, and other items that need gentle handling. Look for tongs with a good grip and a locking mechanism for easy storage.

Basting Cover
This dome-shaped cover traps heat and steam, allowing you to melt cheese, cook burgers faster, and steam vegetables right on the griddle.

Squeeze Bottles
Fill these with oil, water, and your favorite sauces for easy application. They are perfect for controlling the amount of liquid you use, ensuring even distribution.

Meat Thermometer
Ensuring your meat is cooked to the perfect temperature is crucial for both safety and flavor. A reliable digital meat thermometer provides quick and accurate readings.

Grill Press
A heavy-duty grill press helps cook your food evenly and faster by pressing it flat against the griddle surface. It's especially useful for making perfectly crispy bacon and smash burgers.

Cleaning Tools

Griddle Scraper: Essential for removing food residue and keeping your griddle clean.
Scouring Pads: These help remove stubborn grease and burnt-on food.
Grill Brush: A sturdy grill brush with metal bristles helps keep your griddle surface clean and ready for the next use.

Additional Helpful Equipment

Heat-Resistant Gloves
Protect your hands from high temperatures with a good pair of heat-resistant gloves. They provide safety and confidence when handling hot tools and food.

Cutting Board
A durable cutting board is essential for prepping your ingredients. Opt for one that is large enough to handle all your chopping, slicing, and dicing needs.

Mixing Bowls
Have a variety of mixing bowls on hand for marinating meats, mixing batters, and tossing

salads. Stainless steel or glass bowls are versatile and easy to clean.

Storage Containers

Keep your ingredients and leftovers fresh with a set of airtight storage containers. They are also handy for meal prepping and organizing your cooking space.

Knife Set

A high-quality knife set is a must for any kitchen. Ensure you have a chef's knife, paring knife, and serrated knife for all your cutting tasks.

Meat Injector

Enhance the flavor of your meats by injecting marinades and brines directly into them. This tool is perfect for infusing flavor and moisture into your dishes.

Wire Rack

Use a wire rack to rest your cooked food. This prevents the food from becoming soggy by allowing air to circulate around it.

Pastry Brush

A silicone pastry brush is ideal for applying marinades, glazes, and oils to your food, ensuring even coverage without damaging delicate items.

Choosing Quality Equipment

Investing in high-quality tools and equipment will not only improve your cooking results but also make your griddle cooking experience more enjoyable. Here are a few tips for choosing quality equipment:

Durability: Look for tools made from stainless steel, cast iron, or heavy-duty materials that can withstand high temperatures and frequent use.

Ease of Cleaning: Choose tools that are easy to clean and maintain. Dishwasher-safe options save time and effort.

Comfort and Safety: Ergonomic designs with comfortable grips make handling tools easier and safer.

Versatility: Opt for tools that can perform multiple functions to save space and money.

Conclusion

With the right tools and equipment, your gas griddle cooking will reach new heights of efficiency and enjoyment.

How to Choose the Right Gas Griddle

Selecting the perfect gas griddle can significantly enhance your outdoor cooking experience. With numerous options available in the market, it's important to consider various factors to ensure you pick the one that best suits your needs. Here's a comprehensive guide to help you choose the right gas griddle.

Size and Cooking Surface
Assess Your Cooking Needs:

Family Size: If you frequently cook for a large family or enjoy hosting backyard barbecues, opt for a larger griddle with ample cooking space. A griddle with a cooking surface of at least 36 inches will provide enough room to cook multiple items simultaneously.

Compact Options: For smaller families or individuals with limited outdoor space, a compact griddle with a cooking surface of around 22 inches can be an ideal choice. It's also great for tailgating and camping.

Cooking Surface Material:

Cold Rolled Steel: This is the most common material used for gas griddle surfaces. It offers excellent heat retention and distribution, ensuring even cooking. However, it requires regular seasoning to maintain its non-stick properties.

Stainless Steel: While less common, stainless steel griddles are easier to clean and maintain. They are also resistant to rust and corrosion.

Number of Burners
Control and Flexibility:

Multiple Burners: Choose a griddle with multiple burners (at least three) to have better control over different cooking zones. This allows you to cook a variety of foods at different temperatures simultaneously.

Single Burner: If you plan to use your griddle for simple meals or occasional cooking, a single burner griddle might suffice. It's more affordable and easier to manage.

Portability and Storage
Portable Options:

Tabletop Griddles: These are compact, lightweight, and perfect for camping trips or small patios. They can be easily stored away when not in use.

Griddles with Wheels: Larger griddles often come with wheels, making them easier to move around your backyard or patio. Look for models with lockable wheels for added stability during cooking.

Storage Considerations:

Foldable Shelves: Some griddles come with foldable side shelves, providing extra prep space without taking up additional storage room.

Compact Design: If storage space is a concern, opt for a griddle with a slim design that can fit into tight spaces.

Additional Features
Grease Management System:

Built-in Grease Trap: A good grease management system is essential for easy cleanup. Look for griddles with a built-in grease trap or cup that collects excess grease and drippings.

Temperature Control:

Adjustable Heat Controls: Ensure the griddle has easy-to-use temperature control knobs that allow precise heat adjustments for different cooking needs.

Ignition System:

Electronic Ignition: An electronic ignition system provides reliable and quick startup, making it easier to get your griddle ready for cooking.

Lid or Hood:

Optional Lid: Some griddles come with a lid or hood, which can be useful for trapping heat, melting cheese, or protecting the griddle surface when not in use.

Proper Maintenance and Care

Maintaining your gas griddle is essential for ensuring it remains in top condition and continues to deliver exceptional cooking performance. Proper care not only extends the lifespan of your griddle but also ensures safe and efficient operation. Here's a guide to keeping your gas griddle in pristine condition, just like a professional chef would.

Regular Cleaning After Each Use:

Cool Down: Allow the griddle to cool down slightly, but not completely. Cleaning while it's still warm makes removing food residues easier.

Scrape Off Residue: Use a griddle scraper to remove food particles and grease. Scrape from the back to the front, pushing the debris into the grease trap.

Wipe Down: Dampen a paper towel or cloth with water and wipe the griddle surface. Be careful of steam when using water on a warm griddle.

Deep Cleaning:

Soap and Water: For a thorough clean, use warm soapy water and a non-abrasive sponge. Avoid using harsh chemicals or abrasive scrubbers that can damage the griddle surface.

Rinse and Dry: Rinse the surface with clean water and dry it thoroughly with a clean cloth to prevent rusting.

Seasoning Your Griddle
Why Seasoning is Important:

Non-Stick Surface: Seasoning creates a non-stick surface, making cooking and cleaning easier.

Rust Prevention: A well-seasoned griddle is less likely to rust.

How to Season:

Clean the Surface: Start with a clean griddle surface.

Apply Oil: Use a high-smoke-point oil, such as vegetable oil or canola oil. Apply a thin, even layer over the entire surface.

Heat the Griddle: Turn on the griddle and heat it until the oil starts to smoke. This allows the oil to bond with the metal.

Cool and Repeat: Let the griddle cool down and repeat the process 2-3 times to build up a strong seasoning layer.

Grease Management
Grease Trap Maintenance:

Empty Regularly: Frequently empty the grease trap to prevent overflow and maintain cleanliness.

Clean Thoroughly: Remove and clean the grease trap with warm soapy water, ensuring all grease residues are removed.

Protecting Your Griddle
Covering the Griddle:

Use a Cover: When not in use, cover your griddle with a weather-resistant cover to protect it from the elements. This helps prevent rust and keeps debris off the cooking surface.

Store Indoors: If possible, store your griddle indoors, especially during harsh weather conditions.

Solving Common Problems

Even the most seasoned griddle chefs encounter occasional issues while cooking. Understanding how to troubleshoot and solve these common problems ensures that your cooking experience remains smooth and enjoyable. Here are some typical challenges you might face with your gas griddle and effective solutions to keep you griddling like a pro.

Uneven Cooking

Problem: Food cooks unevenly, with some areas more done than others.

Solution:
Preheat Properly: Ensure the griddle is fully preheated before you start cooking. This helps in even heat distribution.
Zone Cooking: Use different areas of the griddle for different heat levels. For instance, the center of the griddle usually gets hotter, so use it for searing while using the edges for slower cooking.
Rotate Food: Rotate or move food around the griddle surface to ensure even cooking, especially for larger items like steaks or pancakes.

Food Sticking to the Griddle

Problem: Food sticks to the griddle surface, making it difficult to flip or remove.

Solution:
Proper Seasoning: Ensure your griddle is well-seasoned. Regular seasoning creates a non-stick surface that prevents food from sticking.
Adequate Oil: Use enough oil or cooking spray before adding food to the griddle. Spread a thin layer of oil evenly across the surface.
Wait to Flip: Allow the food to cook undisturbed until it naturally releases from the griddle. For example, let burgers form a crust before flipping.

Flare-Ups and Excessive Smoke

Problem: Flare-ups or excessive smoke during cooking.

Solution:
Control Grease: Avoid excessive grease buildup by using leaner cuts of meat and trimming excess fat. Also, keep the grease trap clean and empty.
Manage Heat: Use appropriate heat levels for different foods. High heat can cause grease to ignite, leading to flare-ups. Medium heat is usually sufficient for most griddling tasks.
Avoid Overcrowding: Don't overcrowd the griddle surface, as this can lead to uneven cooking and excess grease accumulation, causing flare-ups.

Ignition Problems

Problem: Difficulty igniting the griddle or the flame not staying lit.

Solution:
Check Connections: Ensure the gas connections are secure and the propane tank is not empty. Inspect the hoses for any signs of damage or leaks.
Clean Burners: If the burners are clogged with food debris or grease, clean them thoroughly to ensure proper gas flow.
Battery Replacement: For electronic ignition systems, check and replace the battery if necessary.

Inconsistent Heat

Problem: The griddle doesn't maintain consistent heat, leading to undercooked or overcooked food.

Solution:
Wind Protection: If cooking outdoors, protect the griddle from wind, which can cause heat fluctuations. Use a wind guard if necessary.
Regular Maintenance: Regularly clean and inspect the burners to ensure they're

functioning correctly and providing even heat distribution.

Monitor Gas Levels: Ensure your propane tank has enough gas. Low gas levels can result in inconsistent heat.

Food Tasting Off

Problem: Food has an off taste, possibly due to residues or contamination.

Solution:
Clean Surface: Ensure the griddle is thoroughly cleaned before cooking, especially if it was stored for a while. Use warm soapy water and a non-abrasive scrubber.
Avoid Cross-Contamination: Use separate tools and areas of the griddle for different foods to prevent cross-contamination of flavors.

Tips for Cooking Meat, Fish, Vegetables, and Other Foods

Cooking on a gas griddle offers unparalleled versatility, allowing you to prepare a wide range of foods with precision and flavor. Whether you're grilling a juicy steak, delicate fish, crisp vegetables, or any other ingredient, these tips will help you achieve perfect results every time.

Meat

Steak:

Preheat Properly: Ensure your griddle is fully preheated to high heat to achieve a good sear.
Season Generously: Season steaks with salt, pepper, and any preferred spices just before cooking.

Sear and Cook: Sear steaks for 2-3 minutes on each side to develop a crust, then move to a cooler part of the griddle to finish cooking to your desired doneness.
Rest: Let the steak rest for a few minutes before slicing to allow juices to redistribute.

Chicken:

Flatten Thicker Pieces: Use a meat mallet to flatten chicken breasts for even cooking.
Marinate: Marinate chicken for at least 30 minutes to enhance flavor and tenderness.
Cook Evenly: Grill chicken over medium heat to avoid drying out. Cook until the internal temperature reaches 165°F (75°C).
Turn Once: Turn chicken only once to maintain juiciness and achieve beautiful grill marks.

Pork:

Choose the Right Cuts: Tender cuts like pork chops and tenderloin are best for quick grilling.
Brine or Marinate: Brining or marinating pork adds flavor and moisture.

Monitor Temperature: Use a meat thermometer to cook pork to an internal temperature of 145°F (63°C) for chops and tenderloin, ensuring they remain juicy.

Burgers:

Avoid Overworking: Handle the ground meat gently to keep burgers tender.
Indent the Center: Make a small indentation in the center of each patty to prevent it from puffing up during cooking.
Flip Once: Flip burgers only once to retain juices, cooking them for about 4-5 minutes per side for medium doneness.

Fish

Salmon:

Skin-On: Cook salmon fillets with the skin on to help hold the fish together and prevent sticking.
Preheat and Oil: Preheat the griddle to medium-high heat and oil the surface well.
Cook Skin Side Down: Start with the skin side down and cook for about 4-5 minutes before flipping for an additional 2-3 minutes.

White Fish (e.g., Cod, Halibut):

Season Simply: Use simple seasonings like salt, pepper, and lemon juice to let the fish's flavor shine.
Use a Spatula: Carefully flip the fish using a wide spatula to avoid breaking it apart.
Cook Thoroughly: Cook until the fish is opaque and flakes easily with a fork, about 3-4 minutes per side.

Shrimp:

Quick Cooking: Shrimp cook very quickly, usually in 2-3 minutes per side.
Avoid Overcooking: Remove shrimp from the griddle as soon as they turn pink and opaque to prevent them from becoming rubbery.

Vegetables

Bell Peppers and Onions:

Slice Evenly: Slice vegetables evenly to ensure uniform cooking.
Use High Heat: Grill at high heat to achieve a nice char and caramelization.
Season Lightly: Season with salt, pepper, and a drizzle of olive oil before grilling.

Zucchini and Squash:

Cut Thick: Slice zucchini and squash into thick rounds or lengthwise strips to prevent them from becoming mushy.
Avoid Overcrowding: Give vegetables plenty of space on the griddle to ensure they cook evenly and develop a good char.
Season After Cooking: Season with herbs and a squeeze of lemon juice after grilling for a fresh finish.

Mushrooms:

Use High Heat: Cook mushrooms at high heat to prevent them from releasing too much moisture.
Avoid Overcrowding: Spread mushrooms out on the griddle for even browning.
Finish with Butter: Add a pat of butter towards the end of cooking for added richness.

Other Foods

Pancakes:

Preheat Evenly: Preheat the griddle to medium heat for even cooking.
Use a Ladle: Use a ladle or measuring cup to pour batter for uniform pancakes.
Wait for Bubbles: Flip pancakes once bubbles form on the surface and the edges start to set.

Eggs:

Non-Stick Surface: Ensure the griddle is well-oiled or non-stick before cooking eggs.
Low Heat: Cook eggs over low heat to prevent them from becoming rubbery.
Cover for Steam: Use a basting cover to steam and set the tops of sunny-side-up eggs.

Bacon:

Low and Slow: Cook bacon over medium-low heat to render the fat and achieve crispy strips. Drain Grease: Drain excess grease periodically to prevent splattering and burning.

Quesadillas:

Moderate Heat: Cook quesadillas over medium heat to melt the cheese without burning the tortilla.

Flip Carefully: Use a wide spatula to flip quesadillas, ensuring they stay intact.

By following these tips, you'll be able to achieve perfect results every time, impressing family and friends with your griddle skills.

CHAPTER 2: 30-DAY MEAL PLAN

Day	Breakfast (600 kcal)	Lunch (600 kcal)	Snack (400 kcal)	Dinner (400 kcal)
Day 1	Huevos Rancheros with Grilled Tortillas - p.21	Classic Cheeseburger - p.34	Cheesy Grilled Potatoes - p.48	Grilled Lemon Herb Chicken Breast - p.62
Day 2	Mushroom and Spinach Frittata - p.23	Chicken Alfredo Penne - p.38	Spinach and Artichoke Dip Cups - p.51	Grilled Halibut with Mango Salsa - p.71
Day 3	Breakfast Quesadilla with Bacon and Cheese - p.24	Beef Teriyaki Noodles - p.41	Grilled Pineapple with Honey and Cinnamon - p.55	BBQ Chicken Breast - p.44
Day 4	Fluffy Pancakes with Fresh Berries - p.22	Vegetable Primavera - p.38	Garlic Parmesan Grilled Asparagus - p.49	Grilled Shrimp and Zucchini Boats - p.64
Day 5	Steak and Eggs with Grilled Asparagus - p.30	Spaghetti Carbonara - p.39	Classic Hummus - p.52	Grilled Mahi Mahi with Pineapple Salsa - p.70
Day 6	Breakfast Burrito with Chorizo, Eggs, and Avocado - p.20	Buffalo Chicken Sandwich - p.37	Mini Meatballs - p.51	Classic BBQ Baby Back Ribs - p.73
Day 7	BBQ Pulled Pork Breakfast Tacos - p.29	Chicken Pad Thai - p.42	Grilled Fig and Honey Flatbread - p.58	Grilled Cauliflower Steaks - p.67
Day 8	Sweet Potato and Black Bean Tacos - p.28	Philly Cheesesteak Sandwich - p.36	Tzatziki Sauce - p.54	Herb-Crusted Grilled Tilapia - p.62
Day 9	Protein Pancakes with Almond Butter - p.31	Pesto Pasta with Grilled Chicken - p.39	Buffalo Cauliflower Bites - p.50	Grilled Sirloin Steak with Chimichurri - p.43
Day 10	Grilled Sausage Patties with Eggs and Cheese - p.21	Baked Ziti with Marinara - p.40	Grilled Lemon Bars - p.58	Grilled Pineapple Chicken with Grilled Eggplant and Tomato Salad - p.66
Day 11	Turkey Sausage and Spinach Quesadillas - p.27	Vegetable Fried Rice - p.41	Corn Fritters with Jalapeño - p.48	Lemon Dill Grilled Salmon - p.65
Day 12	Corned Beef Hash with Fried Eggs - p.20	BBQ Bacon Burger - p.34	Baked Jalapeño Poppers - p.50	Honey Garlic Spare Ribs - p.73
Day 13	Ham and Cheese Omelette with Hash Browns - p.22	Pesto Chicken Pizza - p.33	Spinach and Artichoke Dip - p.52	Grilled Zucchini with Parmesan - p.69
Day 14	Grilled Veggie Breakfast Tacos - p.26	Four Cheese Ravioli - p.40	Chocolate Banana Quesadillas - p.55	Herb-Crusted Pork Loin - p.45
Day 15	Huevos Rancheros Tacos - p.25	Spicy Jalapeño Burger - p.37	Griddled Chocolate Chip Cookies - p.57	Maple Glazed Pork Chops - p.44
Day 16	Egg and Sausage Muffins - p.23	Grilled Ribeye Steak - p.43	Queso Dip - p.54	Grilled Tomato and Mozzarella Salad - p.69

Day	Breakfast (600 kcal)	Lunch (600 kcal)	Snack (400 kcal)	Dinner (400 kcal)
Day 17	Shrimp and Avocado Breakfast Tacos - p.28	Balsamic Glazed Steak Tips - p.46	Grilled Strawberry Shortcake - p.57	Paella - p.74
Day 18	Beef and Veggie Breakfast Skillet - p.29	Chicken Caesar Wrap - p.36	Classic Hummus - p.52	Grilled Tuna Steaks with Avocado - p.70
Day 19	Blueberry and Ricotta Breakfast Quesadillas - p.27	Chicken Alfredo Penne - p.38	Crispy Chicken Tenders - p.49	Grilled Meatloaf with Veggies - p.75
Day 20	Ricotta and Berry Crepes - p.31	Grilled Sirloin Steak with Chimichurri - p.43	Grilled Cherry Hand Pies - p.59	Grilled Veggie Platter - p.68
Day 21	Mushroom and Spinach Frittata - p.23	Chicken Pad Thai - p.42	Spinach and Artichoke Dip Cups - p.51	Grilled Swordfish with Tomato Basil Relish - p.71
Day 22	Breakfast Burrito with Chorizo, Eggs, and Avocado - p.20	Philly Cheesesteak Sandwich - p.36	Buffalo Chicken Dip - p.53	Grilled Ribeye Steak - p.43
Day 23	Protein Pancakes with Almond Butter - p.31	Spaghetti Carbonara - p.39	Garlic Parmesan Grilled Asparagus - p.49	Grilled Zucchini Noodles with Pesto - p.67
Day 24	BBQ Pulled Pork Breakfast Tacos - p.29	Four Cheese Ravioli - p.40	Grilled Pineapple with Honey and Cinnamon - p.55	Grilled Tilapia with Garlic Lime Sauce - p.72
Day 25	Ham and Cheese Omelette with Hash Browns - p.22	Pesto Pasta with Grilled Chicken - p.39	Corn Fritters with Jalapeño - p.48	Grilled Lemon Herb Chicken Breast - p.62
Day 26	Grilled Veggie Breakfast Tacos - p.26	Classic Cheeseburger - p.34	Grilled Lemon Bars - p.58	Grilled Shrimp and Zucchini Boats - p.64
Day 27	Steak and Eggs with Grilled Asparagus - p.30	BBQ Chicken Breast - p.44	Classic Hummus - p.52	Maple Glazed Pork Chops - p.44
Day 28	Fluffy Pancakes with Fresh Berries - p.22	Vegetable Fried Rice - p.41	Griddled Chocolate Chip Cookies - p.57	Herb-Crusted Grilled Tilapia - p.62
Day 29	Egg and Sausage Muffins - p.23	Chicken Alfredo Penne - p.38	Baked Jalapeño Poppers - p.50	Honey Garlic Spare Ribs - p.73
Day 30	Sweet Potato and Black Bean Tacos - p.28	Balsamic Glazed Steak Tips - p.46	Spinach and Artichoke Dip - p.52	Grilled Veggie Lasagna - p.75

Note: We'd like to emphasize that the 30-Day Meal Plan provided in this book is meant to be a guiding tool and a source of inspiration. The estimated caloric values of the dishes can vary depending on portion sizes and the specific ingredients used. Our meal plan is crafted to offer a varied and balanced diet, abundant in proteins, healthy fats, and carbohydrates, ensuring you can maintain healthy eating habits without missing out on tasty meals.

If you notice that the calorie counts in the recipes don't completely match your personal requirements or goals, feel free to modify the portion sizes. Adjust them up or down as needed to make the meal plan fit your unique needs and preferences. Use your creativity and enjoy each meal according to what works best for you!

CHAPTER 3: BREAKFASTS: Classic Griddle Breakfasts

Breakfast Burrito with Chorizo, Eggs, and Avocado

Prep: 10 mins | Cook: 15 mins | Serves: 2

Ingredients:

- 2 large tortillas (200g)
- 4 oz chorizo, crumbled (115g)
- 4 large eggs
- 1/4 cup milk (60ml)
- 1 avocado, sliced
- 1/2 cup shredded cheddar cheese (50g)
- 1 tbsp butter (15g)
- Salt and pepper to taste

Instructions:

1. In a skillet, cook chorizo over medium heat until browned. Remove from skillet and set aside.
2. Whisk together eggs, milk, salt, and pepper. In the same skillet, melt butter and scramble the eggs until just set.
3. Warm tortillas on a griddle or in a dry skillet.
4. Assemble burritos by placing chorizo, scrambled eggs, avocado slices, and cheese on each tortilla. Roll up and serve.

Nutritional Facts (Per Serving): Calories: 600 | Carbs: 35g | Protein: 28g | Fat: 40g | Fiber: 6g | Sodium: 1000mg | Sugars: 2g

Corned Beef Hash with Fried Eggs

Prep: 15 mins | Cook: 25 mins | Serves: 2

Ingredients:

- 2 cups diced corned beef (250g)
- 2 cups diced potatoes (300g)
- 1 small onion, diced (70g)
- 1 bell pepper, diced (120g)
- 2 tbsp vegetable oil (30ml)
- 4 large eggs
- Salt and pepper to taste
- Fresh parsley for garnish)

Instructions:

1. Heat oil in a large skillet over medium heat.
2. Add onions and bell peppers, cooking until softened.
3. Add potatoes and cook until browned.
4. Stir in corned beef, cooking until heated through and slightly crispy.
5. In a separate skillet, fry eggs to your liking.
6. Serve corned beef hash topped with fried eggs and garnish with parsley.

Nutritional Facts (Per Serving): Calories: 600 | Carbs: 45g | Protein: 30g | Fat: 35g | Fiber: 5g | Sodium: 1200mg | Sugars: 4g

Grilled Sausage Patties with Eggs and Cheese

Prep: 10 mins | Cook: 20 mins | Serves: 2

Ingredients:

- 4 sausage patties (200g)
- 4 large eggs
- 1/2 cup shredded cheddar cheese (50g)
- 1 tbsp butter (15g)
- Salt and pepper to taste

Instructions:

1. Preheat the griddle over medium heat.
2. Grill the sausage patties until cooked through on each side.
3. In a skillet, melt butter and scramble the eggs with salt and pepper.
4. Serve sausage patties with scrambled eggs and a side of cheddar cheese.

Nutritional Facts (Per Serving): Calories: 600 | Carbs: 4g | Protein: 36g | Fat: 50g | Fiber: 0g | Sodium: 1000mg | Sugars: 1g

Huevos Rancheros with Grilled Tortillas

Prep: 15 mins | Cook: 20 mins | Serves: 2

Ingredients:

- 4 corn tortillas (100g)
- 1 cup black beans, cooked (150g)
- 1 cup spicy tomato salsa (250g)
- 1 avocado, sliced
- 4 large eggs
- 2 tbsp vegetable oil (30ml)
- Salt and pepper to taste
- Fresh cilantro for garnish

Instructions:

1. Heat a griddle over medium-high heat and grill tortillas until warm and slightly charred.
2. Heat oil in a skillet over medium heat and fry eggs to your liking.
3. Warm black beans in a small pot.
4. Assemble by placing tortillas on plates, topping with black beans, fried eggs, salsa, and avocado slices. Garnish with fresh cilantro.

Nutritional Facts (Per Serving): Calories: 600 | Carbs: 60g | Protein: 20g | Fat: 35g | Fiber: 15g | Sodium: 800mg | Sugars: 6g

Fluffy Pancakes with Fresh Berries

Prep: 10 mins | Cook: 20 mins | Serves: 2

Ingredients:

- 1 cup all-purpose flour (120g)
- 1 tbsp sugar (15g)
- 1 tsp baking powder (4g)
- 1/2 tsp baking soda (2g)
- 1/4 tsp salt (1g)
- 3/4 cup buttermilk (180ml)
- 1/4 cup milk (60ml)
- 1 large egg
- 2 tbsp melted butter (30g)
- 1 cup fresh berries (150g)
- Butter or oil for cooking

Instructions:

1. In a bowl, whisk together flour, sugar, baking powder, baking soda, and salt.
2. In another bowl, mix buttermilk, milk, egg, and melted butter.
3. Combine wet and dry ingredients, stirring until just combined.
4. Heat a griddle over medium heat and grease with butter or oil.
5. Pour 1/4 cup batter per pancake onto the griddle. Cook until bubbles form on the surface, then flip and cook until golden brown.
6. Serve pancakes topped with fresh berries.

Nutritional Facts (Per Serving): Calories: 600 | Carbs: 80g | Protein: 15g | Fat: 25g | Fiber: 6g | Sodium: 600mg | Sugars: 20g

Ham and Cheese Omelette with Hash Browns

Prep: 10 mins | Cook: 20 mins | Serves: 2

Ingredients:

- 4 large eggs
- 1/4 cup milk (60ml)
- 1/2 cup diced ham (75g)
- 1/2 cup shredded cheddar cheese (50g)
- 2 tbsp butter (30g)
- Salt and pepper to taste
- 2 cups shredded potatoes (300g)
- 2 tbsp vegetable oil (30ml)

Instructions:

1. Whisk together eggs, milk, salt, and pepper.
2. Heat 1 tbsp butter in a non-stick skillet over medium heat. Pour in half of the egg mixture.
3. When the eggs start to set, sprinkle half of the ham and cheese on one side of the omelette. Fold and cook until cheese melts. Repeat for the second omelette.
4. Heat oil in a large skillet over medium-high heat. Add shredded potatoes, pressing down to form an even layer. Cook until golden and crispy on both sides.
5. Serve omelette with hash browns on the side.

Nutritional Facts (Per Serving): Calories: 600 | Carbs: 35g | Protein: 28g | Fat: 40g | Fiber: 3g | Sodium: 950mg | Sugars: 2g

Mushroom and Spinach Frittata

Prep: 10 mins | Cook: 25 mins | Serves: 2

Ingredients:

- 6 large eggs
- 1/4 cup milk (60ml)
- 1 cup fresh spinach, chopped (30g)
- 1 cup mushrooms, sliced (100g)
- 1/2 cup shredded mozzarella cheese (50g)
- 2 tbsp olive oil (30ml)
- Salt and pepper to taste

Instructions:

1. Preheat the oven to 375°F (190°C).
2. In an oven-safe skillet, heat olive oil over medium heat. Sauté mushrooms until they release their moisture and brown.
3. Add spinach and cook until wilted.
4. In a bowl, whisk together eggs, milk, salt, and pepper. Pour over the vegetables in the skillet. Sprinkle cheese on top.
5. Transfer the skillet to the oven and bake until the frittata is set and golden.
6. Slice and serve.

Nutritional Facts (Per Serving): Calories: 600 | Carbs: 10g | Protein: 30g | Fat: 50g | Fiber: 3g | Sodium: 700mg | Sugars: 4g

Egg and Sausage Muffins

Prep: 10 mins | Cook: 25 mins | Serves: 2

Ingredients:

- 6 large eggs
- 1/4 cup milk (60ml)
- 1/2 cup cooked sausage, crumbled (75g)
- 1/2 cup shredded cheddar cheese (50g)
- 1/4 cup diced bell pepper (30g)
- Salt and pepper to taste
- 1 tbsp butter, melted (15g)

Instructions:

1. Preheat the oven to 375°F (190°C) and grease a muffin tin with melted butter.
2. In a bowl, whisk together eggs, milk, salt, and pepper.
3. Divide sausage, cheese, and bell pepper evenly among muffin cups.
4. Pour egg mixture over the fillings.
5. Bake until the muffins are set and golden.

Nutritional Facts (Per Serving): Calories: 600 | Carbs: 6g | Protein: 36g | Fat: 48g | Fiber: 1g | Sodium: 950mg | Sugars: 2g

CHAPTER 4: BREAKFASTS: Tasty Tacos And Quesadillas

Breakfast Quesadilla with Bacon and Cheese

Prep: 10 mins | Cook: 15 mins | Serves: 2

Ingredients:

- 2 large flour tortillas (200g)
- 4 large eggs
- 1/4 cup milk (60ml)
- 4 strips bacon, cooked and crumbled (60g)
- 1 cup shredded cheddar cheese (100g)
- 1 tbsp butter (15g)
- Salt and pepper to taste

Instructions:

1. Whisk together eggs, milk, salt, and pepper.
2. In a skillet, melt butter over medium heat and scramble the eggs until just set.
3. Heat a griddle over medium heat. Place one tortilla on the griddle, sprinkle with half the cheese, then add scrambled eggs and bacon. Top with remaining cheese and second tortilla.
4. Cook until the tortilla is golden and the cheese is melted, flipping once. Slice into wedges and serve.

Nutritional Facts (Per Serving): Calories: 600 | Carbs: 30g | Protein: 32g | Fat: 40g | Fiber: 2g | Sodium: 1000mg | Sugars: 2g

Spicy Chorizo Breakfast Tacos

Prep: 10 mins | Cook: 15 mins | Serves: 2

Ingredients:

- 4 small corn tortillas (100g)
- 4 oz chorizo, crumbled (115g)
- 4 large eggs
- 1/4 cup milk (60ml)
- 1/4 cup diced onion (40g)
- 1/4 cup chopped fresh cilantro (10g)
- 1/2 cup salsa (120g)
- 1 tbsp vegetable oil (15ml)
- Salt and pepper to taste

Instructions:

1. In a skillet, cook chorizo over medium heat until browned. Remove from skillet and set aside.
2. Whisk together eggs, milk, salt, and pepper. In the same skillet, heat oil and scramble the eggs until just set.
3. Warm tortillas on a griddle or in a dry skillet.
4. Assemble tacos by dividing chorizo and scrambled eggs among the tortillas. Top with onion, cilantro, and salsa.

Nutritional Facts (Per Serving): Calories: 600 | Carbs: 25g | Protein: 30g | Fat: 40g | Fiber: 4g | Sodium: 1100mg | Sugars: 4g

Steak and Cheese Quesadillas

Prep: 10 mins | Cook: 15 mins | Serves: 2

Ingredients:

- 8 oz flank steak, thinly sliced (225g)
- 4 large flour tortillas (200g)
- 1 cup shredded cheddar cheese (100g)
- 1 small onion, sliced (70g)
- 1 bell pepper, sliced (150g)
- 2 tbsp olive oil (30ml)
- 1 tbsp butter (15g)
- Salt and pepper to taste
- Fresh cilantro for garnish (optional) (10g)

Instructions:

1. Heat 1 tbsp olive oil in a skillet over medium-high heat. Season steak with salt and pepper, then cook until browned, about 4-5 minutes. Remove from skillet and set aside.
2. In the same skillet, add remaining olive oil and sauté onion and bell pepper until tender, about 5 minutes.
3. Heat a griddle or large skillet over medium heat. Butter one side of each tortilla.
4. Place a tortilla, buttered side down, on the griddle. Sprinkle with half of the cheese, then add cooked steak, onions, and bell peppers. Top with remaining cheese and second tortilla, buttered side up.
5. Cook until the tortilla is golden and the cheese is melted, flipping once, about 3-4 minutes per side.

6. Slice into wedges and serve, garnished with fresh cilantro if desired.

Nutritional Facts (Per Serving): Calories: 600 | Carbs: 35g | Protein: 32g | Fat: 32g | Fiber: 3g | Sodium: 800mg | Sugars: 4g

Huevos Rancheros Tacos

Prep: 10 mins | Cook: 15 mins | Serves: 2

Ingredients:

- 4 small corn tortillas (100g)
- 4 large eggs
- 1 cup spicy tomato salsa (250g)
- 1 cup black beans, cooked (150g)
- 1 avocado, sliced
- 1 tbsp vegetable oil (15ml)
- Salt and pepper to taste
- Fresh cilantro for garnish (10g)

Instructions:

1. Heat oil in a skillet over medium heat and fry eggs to your liking. Season with salt and pepper.
2. Warm tortillas on a griddle or in a dry skillet.
3. Assemble tacos by placing black beans on each tortilla, followed by a fried egg, salsa, and avocado slices. Garnish with fresh cilantro.

Nutritional Facts (Per Serving): Calories: 600 | Carbs: 42g | Protein: 20g | Fat: 40g | Fiber: 14g | Sodium: 800mg | Sugars: 4g

Grilled Veggie Breakfast Tacos

Prep: 10 mins | Cook: 15 mins | Serves: 2

Ingredients:

- 4 small corn tortillas (100g)
- 1 bell pepper, sliced (150g)
- 1 small onion, sliced (70g)
- 1 small zucchini, sliced (150g)
- 4 large eggs
- 1/4 cup milk (60ml)
- 2 tbsp olive oil (30ml)
- Salt and pepper to taste
- Fresh cilantro for garnish (10g)

Instructions:

1. Heat 1 tbsp olive oil in a skillet over medium heat. Sauté bell pepper, onion, and zucchini until tender. Remove from skillet and set aside.
2. In a bowl, whisk together eggs, milk, salt, and pepper. In the same skillet, heat remaining oil and scramble the eggs until just set.
3. Warm tortillas on a griddle or in a dry skillet.
4. Assemble tacos by placing grilled veggies and scrambled eggs on each tortilla. Garnish with fresh cilantro.

Nutritional Facts (Per Serving): Calories: 600 | Carbs: 38g | Protein: 24g | Fat: 40g | Fiber: 6g | Sodium: 400mg | Sugars: 6g

Pico de Gallo and Avocado Tacos

Prep: 10 mins | Cook: 0 mins | Serves: 2

Ingredients:

- 4 small corn tortillas (100g)
- 1 cup pico de gallo (250g)
- 2 avocados, mashed (400g)
- 1/4 cup queso fresco, crumbled (30g)
- 1 tbsp lime juice (15ml)
- Salt to taste
- Fresh cilantro for garnish (10g)

Instructions:

1. Warm tortillas on a griddle or in a dry skillet.
2. In a bowl, mash avocados with lime juice and salt.
3. Assemble tacos by spreading mashed avocado on each tortilla, topping with pico de gallo and a sprinkle of queso fresco. Garnish with fresh cilantro.

Nutritional Facts (Per Serving): Calories: 600 | Carbs: 40g | Protein: 10g | Fat: 45g | Fiber: 16g | Sodium: 300mg | Sugars: 4g

Turkey Sausage and Spinach Quesadillas

Prep: 10 mins | Cook: 15 mins | Serves: 2

Ingredients:

- 2 large flour tortillas (200g)
- 4 oz turkey sausage, crumbled (115g)
- 1 cup fresh spinach (30g)
- 4 large eggs
- 1/4 cup milk (60ml)
- 1/2 cup shredded cheddar cheese (50g)
- 1 tbsp olive oil (15ml)
- Salt and pepper to taste

Instructions:

1. In a skillet, cook turkey sausage over medium heat until browned. Add spinach and cook until wilted.
2. Whisk together eggs, milk, salt, and pepper. In another skillet, heat half the oil and scramble the eggs until just set. Mix with sausage and spinach.
3. Heat a griddle over medium heat. Place one tortilla on the griddle, sprinkle with half the cheese, then add egg mixture. Top with remaining cheese and second tortilla.
4. Cook until the tortilla is golden and the cheese is melted, flipping once.
5. Slice into wedges and serve.

Nutritional Facts (Per Serving): Calories: 600 | Carbs: 28g | Protein: 38g | Fat: 32g | Fiber: 2g | Sodium: 900mg | Sugars: 2g

Blueberry and Ricotta Breakfast Quesadillas

Prep: 10 mins | Cook: 10 mins | Serves: 2

Ingredients:

- 2 large flour tortillas (200g)
- 1 cup fresh blueberries (150g)
- 1/2 cup ricotta cheese (120g)
- 1 tbsp honey (15ml)
- 1 tsp lemon zest (2g)
- 1 tbsp butter (15g)

Instructions:

1. In a bowl, mix ricotta cheese, honey, and lemon zest.
2. Heat a griddle over medium heat. Butter one side of each tortilla.
3. Place one tortilla, buttered side down, on the griddle. Spread the ricotta mixture over the tortilla, sprinkle with blueberries, and top with the second tortilla, buttered side up.
3. Cook until the tortilla is golden and the cheese is melted, flipping once.
4. Slice into wedges and serve.

Nutritional Facts (Per Serving): Calories: 600 | Carbs: 65g | Protein: 15g | Fat: 28g | Fiber: 5g | Sodium: 300mg | Sugars: 20g

Shrimp and Avocado Breakfast Tacos

Prep: 10 mins | Cook: 10 mins | Serves: 2

Ingredients:

- 4 small corn tortillas (100g)
- 8 oz shrimp, peeled and deveined (225g)
- 1 avocado, sliced (200g)
- 1/4 cup sour cream (60g)
- 1 tbsp lime juice (15ml)
- 1 tsp lime zest (2g)
- 2 tbsp olive oil (30ml)
- Salt and pepper to taste
- Fresh cilantro for garnish (10g)

Instructions:

1. In a bowl, mix sour cream, lime juice, lime zest, salt, and pepper to make the lime crema.
2. Heat olive oil in a skillet over medium heat. Season shrimp with salt and pepper, then grill until pink and cooked through, on each side.
3. Warm tortillas on a griddle or in a dry skillet.
4. Assemble tacos by placing grilled shrimp and avocado slices on each tortilla. Drizzle with lime crema and garnish with fresh cilantro.

Nutritional Facts (Per Serving): Calories: 600 | Carbs: 25g | Protein: 35g | Fat: 40g | Fiber: 10g | Sodium: 600mg | Sugars: 2g

Sweet Potato and Black Bean Tacos

Prep: 10 mins | Cook: 30 mins | Serves: 2

Ingredients:

- 4 small corn tortillas (100g)
- 2 cups sweet potatoes, diced (300g)
- 1 cup black beans, cooked (150g)
- 1/2 cup Greek yogurt (120g)
- 1 tbsp olive oil (15ml)
- 1 tsp cumin (2g)
- 1 tsp paprika (2g)
- Salt and pepper to taste
- Fresh cilantro for garnish (10g)

Instructions:

1. Preheat oven to 400°F (200°C). Toss sweet potatoes with olive oil, cumin, paprika, salt, and pepper. Spread on a baking sheet and roast until tender.
2. Warm tortillas on a griddle or in a dry skillet.
3. Assemble tacos by placing roasted sweet potatoes and black beans on each tortilla. Top with a dollop of Greek yogurt and garnish with fresh cilantro.

Nutritional Facts (Per Serving): Calories: 600 | Carbs: 75g | Protein: 18g | Fat: 20g | Fiber: 18g | Sodium: 500mg | Sugars: 10g

CHAPTER 5: BREAKFASTS: Protein-Packed Breakfasts

BBQ Pulled Pork Breakfast Tacos

Prep: 10 minutes | Cook: 15 minutes | Serves: 2

Ingredients:

- 4 small flour tortillas (200g)
- 1 cup BBQ pulled pork (250g)
- 4 large eggs
- 1/4 cup milk (60ml)
- 1 cup coleslaw (150g)
- 1 tbsp butter (15g)
- Salt and pepper to taste

Instructions:

1. Reheat BBQ pulled pork in a skillet over medium heat until warm.
2. Whisk together eggs, milk, salt, and pepper. In another skillet, melt butter and scramble the eggs until just set.
3. Warm tortillas on a griddle or in a dry skillet.
4. Assemble tacos by placing BBQ pulled pork and scrambled eggs on each tortilla. Top with coleslaw.

Nutritional Facts (Per Serving): Calories: 600 | Carbs: 35g | Protein: 30g | Fat: 35g | Fiber: 3g | Sodium: 800mg | Sugars: 8g

Beef and Veggie Breakfast Skillet

Prep: 10 mins | Cook: 15 mins | Serves: 2

Ingredients:

- 8 oz beef strips (225g)
- 1 cup mixed vegetables (bell peppers, onions, zucchini) (150g)
- 4 large eggs
- 1/4 cup milk (60ml)
- 2 tbsp olive oil (30ml)
- Salt and pepper to taste
- Fresh parsley for garnish (10g)

Instructions:

1. Heat 1 tbsp olive oil in a skillet over medium-high heat. Season beef strips with salt and pepper, then cook until browned. Remove from skillet and set aside.
2. In the same skillet, add remaining olive oil and sauté mixed vegetables until tender.
3. Whisk together eggs, milk, salt, and pepper. Pour over vegetables and scramble until just set.
4. Add beef back to the skillet and stir to combine.
5. Garnish with fresh parsley and serve.

Nutritional Facts (Per Serving): Calories: 600 | Carbs: 10g | Protein: 45g | Fat: 40g | Fiber: 3g | Sodium: 600mg | Sugars: 4g

Steak and Eggs with Grilled Asparagus

Prep: 10 minutes | Cook: 20 minutes | Serves: 2

Ingredients:

- 2 ribeye steaks, 6 oz each (170g each)
- 4 large eggs
- 1 bunch asparagus, trimmed (200g)
- 2 tbsp olive oil (30ml)
- 1 tbsp butter (15g)
- Salt and pepper to taste
- Fresh parsley for garnish (10g)

Instructions:

1. Preheat grill to medium-high heat. Season steaks with salt and pepper, then grill to desired doneness, on each side. Let rest.
2. Toss asparagus with 1 tbsp olive oil, salt, and pepper. Grill until tender.
3. Whisk together eggs, salt, and pepper. In a skillet, heat remaining olive oil and butter, then scramble the eggs until just set.
4. Serve steaks with scrambled eggs and grilled asparagus. Garnish with fresh parsley.

Nutritional Facts (Per Serving): Calories: 600 | Carbs: 5g | Protein: 45g | Fat: 45g | Fiber: 2g | Sodium: 700mg | Sugars: 2g

Grilled Turkey and Veggie Frittata

Prep: 10 mins | Cook: 20 mins | Serves: 2

Ingredients:

- 1 cup grilled turkey breast, diced (150g)
- 1 bell pepper, diced (150g)
- 1 small onion, diced (70g)
- 6 large eggs
- 1/4 cup milk (60ml)
- 1/2 cup shredded mozzarella cheese (50g)
- 2 tbsp olive oil (30ml)
- Salt and pepper to taste

Instructions:

1. Preheat the oven to 375°F (190°C).
2. In an oven-safe skillet, heat olive oil over medium heat. Sauté bell pepper and onion until tender.
3. Add diced turkey to the skillet and cook for 2 minutes.
4. In a bowl, whisk together eggs, milk, salt, and pepper. Pour over the vegetables and turkey in the skillet. Sprinkle cheese on top.
5. Transfer the skillet to the oven and bake until the frittata is set and golden. Slice and serve.

Nutritional Facts (Per Serving): Calories: 600 | Carbs: 10g | Protein: 40g | Fat: 40g | Fiber: 2g | Sodium: 700mg | Sugars: 4g

Protein Pancakes with Almond Butter

Prep: 10 mins | Cook: 15 mins | Serves: 2

Ingredients:

- 1 cup protein pancake mix (120g)
- 1 cup water or milk (240ml)
- 2 tbsp almond butter (30g)
- 1 banana, sliced (120g)
- 1 tbsp butter (15g)
- 1 tsp vanilla extract (5ml) (optional)

Instructions:

1. In a bowl, mix protein pancake mix with water or milk, and vanilla extract if using.
2. Heat a griddle over medium heat and melt butter.
3. Pour 1/4 cup batter per pancake onto the griddle. Cook until bubbles form on the surface, then flip and cook until golden brown.
4. Top pancakes with almond butter and sliced bananas.

Nutritional Facts (Per Serving): Calories: 600 | Carbs: 60g | Protein: 30g | Fat: 25g | Fiber: 6g | Sodium: 500mg | Sugars: 14g

Ricotta and Berry Crepes

Prep: 10 mins | Cook: 20 mins | Serves: 2

Ingredients:

- 1 cup all-purpose flour (120g)
- 2 large eggs
- 1/2 cup milk (120ml)
- 1/2 cup water (120ml)
- 1/4 tsp salt (1g)
- 2 tbsp butter, melted (30g)
- 1/2 cup ricotta cheese (120g)
- 1 cup mixed fresh berries (150g)
- 1 tbsp powdered sugar (15g)

Instructions:

1. In a bowl, whisk together flour, eggs, milk, water, and salt until smooth. Let batter rest for 10 minutes.
2. Heat a lightly oiled griddle or frying pan over medium-high heat. Pour 1/4 cup of batter onto the griddle for each crepe, tilting the pan to spread the batter evenly.
3. Cook crepe until the bottom is light brown. Loosen with a spatula, flip and cook the other side.
4. Fill crepes with ricotta cheese and berries. Fold and sprinkle with powdered sugar.

Nutritional Facts (Per Serving): Calories: 600 | Carbs: 70g | Protein: 18g | Fat: 26g | Fiber: 5g | Sodium: 400mg | Sugars: 20g

Classic Margherita Pizza

Prep: 10 mins | Cook: 15 mins | Serves: 2

Ingredients:

- 1 pre-made pizza crust (200g)
- 1/2 cup tomato sauce (120ml)
- 1 cup fresh mozzarella, sliced (150g)
- 1/4 cup fresh basil leaves (10g)
- 2 tbsp olive oil (30ml)
- Salt and pepper to taste

Instructions:

1. Preheat oven to 475°F (245°C).
2. Spread tomato sauce evenly over the pizza crust.
3. Arrange mozzarella slices on top of the sauce.
4. Drizzle with olive oil and season with salt and pepper.
5. Bake in the preheated oven until the crust is golden and the cheese is bubbly.
6. Remove from oven and scatter fresh basil leaves over the top before serving.

Nutritional Facts (Per Serving): Calories: 600 | Carbs: 50g | Protein: 25g | Fat: 30g | Fiber: 2g | Sodium: 900mg | Sugars: 4g

Pepperoni Delight Pizza

Prep: 10 mins | Cook: 15 mins | Serves: 2

Ingredients:

- 1 pre-made pizza crust (200g)
- 1/2 cup tomato sauce (120ml)
- 1 cup shredded mozzarella cheese (100g)
- 1/2 cup sliced pepperoni (75g)
- 1/4 cup grated Parmesan cheese (25g)
- 1 tbsp olive oil (15ml)
- 1 tsp dried oregano (2g)
- Salt and pepper to taste

Instructions:

1. Preheat oven to 475°F (245°C).
2. Spread tomato sauce evenly over the pizza crust.
3. Sprinkle shredded mozzarella cheese over the sauce.
4. Arrange pepperoni slices on top of the cheese.
5. Sprinkle grated Parmesan cheese and dried oregano over the pepperoni.
6. Drizzle with olive oil and season with salt and pepper.
7 Bake in the preheated oven until the crust is golden and the cheese is bubbly. Slice and serve.

Nutritional Facts (Per Serving): Calories: 600 | Carbs: 40g | Protein: 28g | Fat: 32g | Fiber: 2g | Sodium: 1000mg | Sugars: 4g

Pesto Chicken Pizza

Prep: 10 mins | Cook: 15 mins | Serves: 2

Ingredients:

- 1 pre-made pizza crust (200g)
- 1/2 cup pesto sauce (120ml)
- 1 cup cooked chicken breast, diced (150g)
- 1 cup shredded mozzarella cheese (100g)
- 1/4 cup grated Parmesan cheese (25g)
- 1/4 cup cherry tomatoes, halved (40g)
- 1 tbsp olive oil (15ml)
- Salt and pepper to taste

Instructions:

1. Preheat oven to 475°F (245°C).
2. Spread pesto sauce evenly over the pizza crust.
3. Sprinkle shredded mozzarella cheese over the pesto.
4. Arrange diced chicken and cherry tomatoes on top of the cheese.
5. Sprinkle grated Parmesan cheese over the toppings.
6. Drizzle with olive oil and season with salt and pepper.
7. Bake in the preheated oven until the crust is golden and the cheese is bubbly, about 10-12 minutes.Slice and serve.

Nutritional Facts (Per Serving): Calories: 600 | Carbs: 35g | Protein: 35g | Fat: 30g | Fiber: 2g | Sodium: 800mg | Sugars: 3g

Hawaiian Paradise Pizza

Prep: 10 mins | Cook: 15 mins | Serves: 2

Ingredients:

- 1 pre-made pizza crust (200g)
- 1/2 cup tomato sauce (120ml)
- 1 cup shredded mozzarella cheese (100g)
- 1/2 cup cooked ham, diced (75g)
- 1/2 cup pineapple chunks (75g)
- 1/4 cup red onion, thinly sliced (30g)
- 1 tbsp olive oil (15ml)
- Salt and pepper to taste

Instructions:

1. Preheat oven to 475°F (245°C).
2. Spread tomato sauce evenly over the pizza crust.
3. Sprinkle shredded mozzarella cheese over the sauce.
4. Arrange diced ham, pineapple chunks, and red onion slices on top of the cheese.
5. Drizzle with olive oil and season with salt and pepper.
6. Bake in the preheated oven until the crust is golden and the cheese is bubbly, about 10-12 minutes.
7. Slice and serve.

Nutritional Facts (Per Serving): Calories: 600 | Carbs: 45g | Protein: 25g | Fat: 28g | Fiber: 3g | Sodium: 900mg | Sugars: 10g

Classic Cheeseburger

Prep: 15 mins | Cook: 10 mins | Serves: 4

Ingredients:

- 1 lb ground beef (450g)
- 4 slices cheddar cheese (120g)
- 4 lettuce leaves
- 4 tomato slices
- 4 dill pickles
- 4 toasted buns
- Salt and pepper to taste

Instructions:

1. Form ground beef into four equal patties and season with salt and pepper.
2. Grill patties over medium-high heat for 3-4 minutes per side or until desired doneness.
3. During the last minute of cooking, place a slice of cheddar cheese on each patty to melt.
4. Assemble burgers by placing each patty on a toasted bun, topping with lettuce, tomato, and pickles.

Nutritional Facts (Per Serving): Calories: 600 | Sugars: 5g | Fat: 35g | Carbohydrates: 35g | Protein: 30g | Fiber: 2g | Sodium: 1000mg

BBQ Bacon Burger

Prep: 15 mins | Cook: 15 mins | Serves: 4

Ingredients:

- 1 lb ground beef (450g)
- 8 slices crispy bacon (200g)
- 4 slices sharp cheddar cheese (120g)
- 4 tbsp BBQ sauce (60g)
- 4 toasted buns
- Salt and pepper to taste

Instructions:

1. Form ground beef into four equal patties and season with salt and pepper.
2. Grill patties over medium-high heat for 3-4 minutes per side or until desired doneness.
3. During the last minute of cooking, place a slice of sharp cheddar cheese on each patty to melt.
4. Assemble burgers by placing each patty on a toasted bun, topping with 2 slices of crispy bacon and 1 tbsp of BBQ sauce.

Nutritional Facts (Per Serving): Calories: 600 | Sugars: 10g | Fat: 40g | Carbohydrates: 30g | Protein: 28g | Fiber: 1g | Sodium: 1200mg

Mushroom Swiss Burger

Prep: 15 mins | Cook: 10 mins | Serves: 4

Ingredients:

- 1 lb ground beef (450g)
- 8 oz sliced mushrooms (225g)
- 4 slices Swiss cheese (120g)
- 4 toasted buns
- 2 tbsp butter (30g)
- Salt and pepper to taste

Instructions:

1. Form ground beef into four equal patties and season with salt and pepper.
2. Grill patties over medium-high heat for 3-4 minutes per side or until desired doneness.
3. In a pan, melt butter and sauté mushrooms until tender, about 5 minutes.
4. During the last minute of cooking, place a slice of Swiss cheese on each patty to melt.
5. Assemble burgers by placing each patty on a toasted bun and topping with sautéed mushrooms.

Nutritional Facts (Per Serving): Calories: 600 | Sugars: 4g | Fat: 35g | Carbohydrates: 30g | Protein: 28g | Fiber: 2g | Sodium: 800mg

Turkey Avocado Club Sandwich

Prep: 10 mins | Cook: 5 mins | Serves: 4

Ingredients:

- 12 oz sliced turkey (340g)
- 1 avocado, sliced (150g)
- 8 slices bacon (200g)
- 4 lettuce leaves
- 8 tomato slices
- 8 slices whole wheat bread (320g)
- Salt and pepper to taste

Instructions:

1. Toast the whole wheat bread slices.
2. Cook bacon until crispy, about 5 minutes.
3. Assemble sandwiches by layering turkey, avocado slices, bacon, lettuce, and tomato between two slices of toasted bread.
4. Season with salt and pepper to taste.

Nutritional Facts (Per Serving): Calories: 600 | Sugars: 6g | Fat: 28g | Carbohydrates: 45g | Protein: 30g | Fiber: 8g | Sodium: 900mg

Chicken Caesar Wrap

Prep: 10 mins | Cook: 10 mins | Serves: 4

Ingredients:

- 2 grilled chicken breasts, sliced (300g)
- 4 cups chopped romaine lettuce (200g)
- 1/2 cup grated Parmesan cheese (50g)
- 1/2 cup Caesar dressing (120g)
- 4 whole wheat wraps (240g)

Instructions:

1. In a bowl, toss the romaine lettuce with Caesar dressing.
2. Place a portion of grilled chicken slices and dressed romaine lettuce onto each whole wheat wrap.
3. Sprinkle with grated Parmesan cheese.
4. Roll up the wraps tightly and slice in half to serve.

Nutritional Facts (Per Serving): Calories: 600 | Sugars: 4g | Fat: 32g | Carbohydrates: 38g | Protein: 38g | Fiber: 6g | Sodium: 1200mg

Philly Cheesesteak Sandwich

Prep: 15 mins | Cook: 15 mins | Serves: 4

Ingredients:

- 1 lb thinly sliced steak (450g)
- 1 large onion, sliced (150g)
- 1 large green bell pepper, sliced (150g)
- 8 slices provolone cheese (200g)
- 4 hoagie rolls (400g)
- 2 tbsp olive oil (30g)
- Salt and pepper to taste

Instructions:

1. Heat olive oil in a large skillet over medium-high heat.
2. Sauté onions and bell peppers until tender, about 5-7 minutes.
3. Add thinly sliced steak to the skillet, seasoning with salt and pepper. Cook until browned, about 5 minutes.
4. Place a portion of the steak and vegetable mixture onto each hoagie roll and top with 2 slices of provolone cheese.
5. Place the sandwiches under a broiler until the cheese is melted and bubbly.

Nutritional Facts (Per Serving): Calories: 600 | Sugars: 5g | Fat: 30g | Carbohydrates: 45g | Protein: 34g | Fiber: 4g | Sodium: 1000mg

Spicy Jalapeño Burger

Prep: 15 mins | Cook: 10 mins | Serves: 4

Ingredients:

- 1 lb ground beef (450g)
- 2 fresh jalapeños, sliced (30g)
- 4 slices pepper jack cheese (120g)
- 4 tbsp Greek yogurt (60g)
- 4 toasted buns
- Salt and pepper to taste

Instructions:

1. Form ground beef into four equal patties and season with salt and pepper.
2. Grill patties over medium-high heat for 3-4 minutes per side or until desired doneness.
3. During the last minute of cooking, place a slice of pepper jack cheese on each patty to melt.
4. Assemble burgers by placing each patty on a toasted bun, topping with sliced jalapeños and a dollop of Greek yogurt.

Nutritional Facts (Per Serving): Calories: 600 | Sugars: 3g | Fat: 35g | Carbohydrates: 30g | Protein: 32g | Fiber: 2g | Sodium: 850mg

Buffalo Chicken Sandwich

Prep: 10 mins | Cook: 10 mins | Serves: 4

Ingredients:

- 4 grilled chicken breasts (600g)
- 1/2 cup buffalo sauce (120g)
- 4 lettuce leaves
- 4 tbsp blue cheese dressing (60g)
- 4 toasted buns
- Salt and pepper to taste

Instructions:

1. Grill chicken breasts over medium heat until fully cooked, about 5 minutes per side.
2. Toss cooked chicken breasts in buffalo sauce.
3. Assemble sandwiches by placing each buffalo chicken breast on a toasted bun, topping with a lettuce leaf and 1 tbsp of blue cheese dressing.

Nutritional Facts (Per Serving): Calories: 600 | Sugars: 4g | Fat: 28g | Carbohydrates: 35g | Protein: 40g | Fiber: 2g | Sodium: 1100mg

Chicken Alfredo Penne

Prep: 10 mins | Cook: 15 mins | Serves: 4

Ingredients:

- 8 oz penne pasta (225g)
- 2 grilled chicken breasts, sliced (300g)
- 1 cup heavy cream (240ml)
- 1/2 cup grated Parmesan cheese (50g)
- 2 tbsp butter (30g)
- 2 cloves garlic, minced (10g)
- Salt and pepper to taste

Instructions:

1. Cook penne pasta according to package instructions.
2. In a pan, melt butter over medium heat and sauté minced garlic until fragrant, about 1 minute.
3. Add heavy cream and bring to a simmer. Stir in Parmesan cheese until melted and the sauce thickens.
4. Toss the cooked penne pasta and sliced grilled chicken in the Alfredo sauce. Season with salt and pepper.

Nutritional Facts (Per Serving): Calories: 600 | Sugars: 2g | Fat: 35g | Carbohydrates: 45g | Protein: 30g | Fiber: 2g | Sodium: 800mg

Vegetable Primavera

Prep: 10 mins | Cook: 15 mins | Serves: 4

Ingredients:

- 8 oz penne pasta (225g)
- 1 zucchini, sliced (150g)
- 1 bell pepper, sliced (150g)
- 2 tomatoes, diced (200g)
- 2 tbsp olive oil (30ml)
- 2 cloves garlic, minced (10g)
- Salt and pepper to taste
- Fresh basil for garnish

Instructions:

1. Cook penne pasta according to package instructions.
2. In a large pan, heat olive oil over medium heat and sauté minced garlic until fragrant, about 1 minute.
3. Add sliced zucchini, bell pepper, and tomatoes. Cook until vegetables are tender, about 5-7 minutes.
4. Toss the cooked penne pasta with the vegetable mixture. Season with salt and pepper. Garnish with fresh basil.

Nutritional Facts (Per Serving): Calories: 600 | Sugars: 7g | Fat: 20g | Carbohydrates: 80g | Protein: 15g | Fiber: 6g | Sodium: 400mg

Spaghetti Carbonara

Prep: 10 mins | Cook: 15 mins | Serves: 4

Ingredients:

- 12 oz spaghetti (340g)
- 4 oz pancetta, diced (115g)
- 2 large eggs (100g)
- 1 cup grated Parmesan cheese (100g)
- 2 cloves garlic, minced (10g)
- Salt and pepper to taste

Instructions:

1. Cook spaghetti according to package instructions.
2. In a pan, cook diced pancetta over medium heat until crispy, about 5 minutes. Add minced garlic and cook for 1 minute.
3. In a bowl, whisk eggs and grated Parmesan cheese together.
4. Drain the spaghetti and return to the pan with pancetta. Remove from heat and quickly stir in the egg and cheese mixture, tossing to coat the pasta. Season with salt and pepper.

Nutritional Facts (Per Serving): Calories: 600 | Sugars: 2g | Fat: 24g | Carbohydrates: 70g | Protein: 28g | Fiber: 3g | Sodium: 800mg

Pesto Pasta with Grilled Chicken

Prep: 10 mins | Cook: 15 mins | Serves: 4

Ingredients:

- 8 oz penne pasta (225g)
- 2 grilled chicken breasts, sliced (300g)
- 1/2 cup basil pesto (120g)
- 1/4 cup grated Parmesan cheese (25g)
- 2 tbsp olive oil (30ml)
- Salt and pepper to taste

Instructions:

1. Cook penne pasta according to package instructions.
2. Slice grilled chicken breasts.
3. In a large bowl, toss the cooked penne pasta with basil pesto, sliced grilled chicken, and grated Parmesan cheese. Drizzle with olive oil and season with salt and pepper.

Nutritional Facts (Per Serving): Calories: 600 | Sugars: 2g | Fat: 28g | Carbohydrates: 50g | Protein: 34g | Fiber: 3g | Sodium: 600mg

Baked Ziti with Marinara

Prep: 10 mins | Cook: 30 mins | Serves: 4

Ingredients:

- 8 oz ziti pasta (225g)
- 2 cups marinara sauce (480ml)
- 1 cup ricotta cheese (250g)
- 1 1/2 cups shredded mozzarella cheese (150g)
- 1/4 cup grated Parmesan cheese (25g)
- Salt and pepper to taste

Instructions:

1. Preheat oven to 375°F (190°C). Cook ziti pasta according to package instructions.
2. In a bowl, mix cooked ziti with marinara sauce and ricotta cheese.
3. Transfer mixture to a baking dish, top with shredded mozzarella and Parmesan cheese.
4. Bake for 20-25 minutes until cheese is melted and bubbly.

Nutritional Facts (Per Serving): Calories: 600 | Sugars: 8g | Fat: 28g | Carbohydrates: 62g | Protein: 28g | Fiber: 5g | Sodium: 900mg

Four Cheese Ravioli

Prep: 10 mins | Cook: 10 mins | Serves: 4

Ingredients:

- 1 lb four cheese ravioli (450g)
- 2 cups tomato basil sauce (480ml)
- 1/2 cup shredded mozzarella cheese (50g)
- 1/2 cup grated Parmesan cheese (50g)
- 1/4 cup grated Pecorino Romano cheese (25g)
- 1/4 cup ricotta cheese (50g)
- Fresh basil for garnish

Instructions:

1. Cook four cheese ravioli according to package instructions.
2. In a large pan, heat tomato basil sauce over medium heat.
3. Add cooked ravioli to the pan and toss gently to coat.
4. Serve ravioli topped with shredded mozzarella, grated Parmesan, Pecorino Romano, and dollops of ricotta cheese. Garnish with fresh basil.

Nutritional Facts (Per Serving): Calories: 600 | Sugars: 10g | Fat: 30g | Carbohydrates: 58g | Protein: 24g | Fiber: 4g | Sodium: 1000mg

Vegetable Fried Rice

Prep: 10 mins | Cook: 15 mins | Serves: 4

Ingredients:

- 2 cups cooked rice (370g)
- 1 cup frozen peas (150g)
- 1 cup diced carrots (150g)
- 1 bell pepper, diced (150g)
- 2 eggs, scrambled (100g)
- 2 tbsp soy sauce (30ml)
- 2 tbsp vegetable oil (30ml)
- 2 cloves garlic, minced (10g)
- Salt and pepper to taste

Instructions:

1. Heat vegetable oil in a large skillet or wok over medium-high heat.
2. Add minced garlic, diced carrots, and bell pepper. Stir-fry until vegetables are tender, about 5 minutes.
3. Add cooked rice, frozen peas, and scrambled eggs to the skillet. Stir-fry for another 5 minutes.
4. Stir in soy sauce, salt, and pepper. Cook for an additional 2 minutes.

Nutritional Facts (Per Serving): Calories: 600 | Sugars: 5g | Fat: 18g | Carbohydrates: 90g | Protein: 16g | Fiber: 5g | Sodium: 800mg

Beef Teriyaki Noodles

Prep: 10 mins | Cook: 20 mins | Serves: 4

Ingredients:

- 8 oz beef sirloin, thinly sliced (225g)
- 8 oz noodles (225g)
- 1 cup broccoli florets (150g)
- 1 bell pepper, sliced (150g)
- 1/2 cup teriyaki sauce (120ml)
- 2 tbsp vegetable oil (30ml)
- 2 cloves garlic, minced (10g)
- 1 tbsp sesame seeds (15g)
- Salt and pepper to taste

Instructions:

1. Cook noodles according to package instructions.
2. In a large skillet or wok, heat vegetable oil over medium-high heat. Add minced garlic and sliced beef. Cook until beef is browned, about 5 minutes.
3. Add broccoli florets and sliced bell pepper. Stir-fry until vegetables are tender, about 5-7 minutes.
4. Stir in cooked noodles and teriyaki sauce. Cook for another 3 minutes.
5. Garnish with sesame seeds. Season with salt and pepper to taste.

Nutritional Facts (Per Serving): Calories: 600 | Sugars: 12g | Fat: 20g | Carbohydrates: 70g | Protein: 28g | Fiber: 4g | Sodium: 1000mg

Pineapple Fried Rice

Prep: 10 mins | Cook: 15 mins | Serves: 4

Ingredients:

- 2 cups cooked rice (370g)
- 1 cup diced pineapple (150g)
- 1 bell pepper, diced (150g)
- 1/2 cup cashews (75g)
- 2 eggs, scrambled (100g)
- 2 tbsp soy sauce (30ml)
- 2 tbsp vegetable oil (30ml)
- 2 cloves garlic, minced (10g)
- Salt and pepper to taste

Instructions:

1. Heat vegetable oil in a large skillet or wok over medium-high heat.
2. Add minced garlic and diced bell pepper. Stir-fry until vegetables are tender, about 5 minutes.
3. Add cooked rice, diced pineapple, and scrambled eggs to the skillet. Stir-fry for another 5 minutes.
4. Stir in soy sauce and cashews. Cook for an additional 2 minutes. Season with salt and pepper.

Nutritional Facts (Per Serving): Calories: 600 | Sugars: 10g | Fat: 22g | Carbohydrates: 85g | Protein: 14g | Fiber: 5g | Sodium: 800mg

Chicken Pad Thai

Prep: 15 mins | Cook: 15 mins | Serves: 4

Ingredients:

- 8 oz rice noodles (225g)
- 2 grilled chicken breasts, sliced (300g)
- 1 cup bean sprouts (100g)
- 1/2 cup crushed peanuts (75g)
- 1/4 cup tamarind paste (60g)
- 2 tbsp fish sauce (30ml)
- 2 tbsp low carb sweeteners (30g)
- 2 tbsp vegetable oil (30ml)
- 2 cloves garlic, minced (10g)
- 2 eggs, scrambled (100g)
- 1 lime, cut into wedges
- Fresh cilantro for garnish
- Salt and pepper to taste

Instructions:

1. Cook rice noodles as per package instructions, drain.
2. Heat oil in a skillet over medium-high heat, sauté garlic for 1 min.
3. Add chicken and eggs, stir-fry for 2 mins.
4. Stir in tamarind paste, fish sauce, and low carb sweeteners. Add cooked noodles and toss to coat evenly.
5. Add bean sprouts and cook for another 2 minutes. Garnish with crushed peanuts, fresh cilantro, and lime wedges. Season with salt and pepper.

Nutritional Facts (Per Serving): Calories: 600 | Sugars: 8g | Fat: 22g | Carbohydrates: 70g | Protein: 28g | Fiber: 4g | Sodium: 900mg

CHAPTER 10: LUNCHES: Hearty Mains and Steaks

Grilled Ribeye Steak

Prep: 10 mins | Cook: 20 mins | Serves: 4

Ingredients:

- 4 ribeye steaks (8 oz each) (225g each)
- 1/2 cup unsalted butter, softened (115g)
- 4 cloves garlic, minced (20g)
- 2 tbsp fresh parsley, chopped (8g)
- Salt and pepper to taste
- 2 lbs russet potatoes, peeled and diced (900g)
- 1/2 cup milk (120ml)
- 4 tbsp butter (60g)
- 1 lb green beans, trimmed (450g)

Instructions:

1. Preheat grill to medium-high heat. Season ribeye steaks with salt and pepper.

2. In a bowl, mix softened butter with minced garlic and chopped parsley. Set aside.

3. Grill steaks for 5-7 minutes per side or until desired doneness. Top each steak with a dollop of garlic butter before serving.

4. Boil potatoes until tender, about 15 minutes. Drain and mash with milk and butter. Season with salt and pepper.

5. Steam green beans until tender.

Nutritional Facts (Per Serving): Calories: 600 | Sugars: 3g | Fat: 35g | Carbohydrates: 45g | Protein: 30g | Fiber: 5g | Sodium: 800mg

Grilled Sirloin Steak with Chimichurri

Prep: 15 mins | Cook: 25 mins | Serves: 4

Ingredients:

- 4 sirloin steaks (6 oz each) (170g each)
- 1 cup fresh parsley, chopped (60g)
- 1/2 cup olive oil (120ml)
- 1/4 cup red wine vinegar (60ml)
- 4 cloves garlic, minced (20g)
- 1 tsp red pepper flakes (5g)
- Salt and pepper to taste
- 4 ears corn on the cob
- 1 cup long-grain rice (200g)
- 2 cups chicken broth (480ml)
- 1 small onion, chopped (100g)

Instructions:

1. Preheat grill to medium-high heat. Season sirloin steaks with salt and pepper.

2. In a bowl, mix chopped parsley, olive oil, red wine vinegar, minced garlic, and red pepper flakes to make chimichurri sauce.

3. Grill steaks for 5-7 minutes per side or until desired doneness. Let rest before slicing. Top with chimichurri sauce.

4. Grill corn on the cob until charred, about 10 minutes, turning occasionally.

5. In a pot, cook chopped onion in a little oil until soft. Add rice and chicken broth. Bring to a boil, then simmer for 15 minutes or until rice is tender.

Nutritional Facts (Per Serving): Calories: 600 | Sugars: 4g | Fat: 30g | Carbohydrates: 50g | Protein: 28g | Fiber: 5g | Sodium: 700mg

Maple Glazed Pork Chops

Prep: 10 mins | Cook: 25 mins | Serves: 4

Ingredients:

- 4 pork chops (6 oz each) (170g each)
- 1/2 cup maple syrup (120ml)
- 2 tbsp Dijon mustard (30g)
- 2 lbs sweet potatoes, peeled and diced (900g)
- 2 tbsp olive oil (30ml)
- 1 lb green beans, trimmed (450g)
- 2 cloves garlic, minced (10g)
- Salt and pepper to taste

Instructions:

1. Preheat oven to 400°F (200°C). Toss diced sweet potatoes with olive oil, salt, and pepper. Roast for 20-25 minutes or until tender.

2. Preheat grill to medium-high heat. Season pork chops with salt and pepper.

3. In a bowl, mix maple syrup and Dijon mustard. Grill pork chops for 5-7 minutes per side, brushing with maple glaze during the last few minutes.

4. In a pan, sauté green beans with minced garlic until tender, about 5 minutes. Season with salt and pepper.

Nutritional Facts (Per Serving): Calories: 600 | Sugars: 18g | Fat: 22g | Carbohydrates: 55g | Protein: 38g | Fiber: 8g | Sodium: 700mg

BBQ Chicken Breast

Prep: 10 mins | Cook: 20 mins | Serves: 4

Ingredients:

- 4 chicken breasts (6 oz each) (170g each)
- 1 cup BBQ sauce (240ml)
- 1/2 head cabbage, shredded (300g)
- 2 carrots, grated (100g)
- 1/4 cup Greek yogurt (60g)
- 2 tbsp apple cider vinegar (30ml)
- 1 tbsp low carb sweeteners (15g)
- 4 pieces cornbread (120g each)

Instructions:

1. Preheat grill to medium-high heat. Season chicken breasts with salt and pepper.

2. Grill chicken breasts for 6-8 minutes per side, brushing with BBQ sauce during the last few minutes.

3. In a bowl, mix shredded cabbage, grated carrots, Greek yogurt, apple cider vinegar, and low carb sweeteners. Season with salt and pepper to taste.

4. Serve grilled BBQ chicken breasts with a side of coleslaw and a piece of cornbread.

Nutritional Facts (Per Serving): Calories: 600 | Sugars: 14g | Fat: 20g | Carbohydrates: 55g | Protein: 38g | Fiber: 5g | Sodium: 800mg

Herb-Crusted Pork Loin

Prep: 15 mins | Cook: 30 mins | Serves: 4

Ingredients:

- 1.5 lbs pork loin (680g)
- 1/4 cup fresh parsley, chopped (15g)
- 2 tbsp fresh rosemary, chopped (8g)
- 2 tbsp fresh thyme, chopped (8g)
- 4 cloves garlic, minced (20g)
- 2 tbsp olive oil (30ml)
- Salt and pepper to taste
- 1 lb baby carrots (450g)
- 1 cup quinoa (185g)
- 2 cups vegetable broth (480ml)
- 1/4 cup red onion, finely chopped (40g)
- 1/4 cup fresh parsley, chopped (15g)
- 1 tbsp lemon juice (15ml)

Instructions:

1. Preheat grill to medium-high heat. Mix parsley, rosemary, thyme, garlic, olive oil, salt, and pepper. Rub mixture over pork loin.

2. Grill pork loin for 20-25 minutes, turning occasionally, until internal temperature reaches 145°F (63°C). Let rest for 5 minutes before slicing.

3. Toss baby carrots with olive oil, salt, and pepper. Roast in oven at 400°F (200°C) for 20-25 minutes.

4. Cook quinoa in vegetable broth according to package instructions. Mix cooked quinoa with red onion, parsley, and lemon juice.

Nutritional Facts (Per Serving): Calories: 600 | Sugars: 7g | Fat: 24g | Carbohydrates: 45g | Protein: 45g | Fiber: 6g | Sodium: 600mg

Beef Tenderloin with Mushroom Sauce

Prep: 15 mins | Cook: 25 mins | Serves: 4

Ingredients:

- 4 beef tenderloin steaks (6 oz each) (170g each)
- 2 tbsp olive oil (30ml)
- Salt and pepper to taste
- 8 oz mushrooms, sliced (225g)
- 1/2 cup beef broth (120ml)
- 1/4 cup heavy cream (60ml)
- 2 cloves garlic, minced (10g)
- 1 cup polenta (160g)
- 4 cups water (960ml)
- 1/2 cup grated Parmesan cheese (50g)
- 1 tbsp butter (15g)
- 1 lb spinach, sautéed (450g)

Instructions:

1. Preheat oven to 400°F (200°C). Season beef tenderloin with salt and pepper. Heat olive oil in a

skillet over medium-high heat and sear steaks for 2-3 minutes per side. Transfer to oven and roast for 10-15 minutes for medium-rare.

2. In the same skillet, sauté mushrooms and garlic until tender, about 5 minutes. Add beef broth and cream, simmer for 5 minutes until sauce thickens.

3. Cook polenta in water according to package instructions. Stir in Parmesan cheese and butter.

4. Sauté spinach with olive oil, salt, and pepper until wilted, about 3 minutes.

Nutritional Facts (Per Serving): Calories: 600 | Sugars: 4g | Fat: 30g | Carbohydrates: 45g | Protein: 38g | Fiber: 5g | Sodium: 700mg

Grilled Chicken and Vegetable Skewers

Prep: 15 mins | Cook: 20 mins | Serves: 4

Ingredients:

- 1.5 lbs chicken breasts, cubed (680g)
- 2 bell peppers, diced (300g)
- 1 large onion, diced (150g)
- 2 zucchinis, sliced (300g)
- 1 cup couscous (170g)
- 2 cups chicken broth (480ml)
- 1 cup tzatziki sauce (240ml)
- 2 tbsp olive oil (30ml)
- 2 cloves garlic, minced (10g)
- Salt and pepper to taste

Instructions:

1. Preheat grill to medium-high heat. Thread chicken, bell peppers, onions, and zucchinis onto skewers.

2. Brush skewers with olive oil and minced garlic. Season with salt and pepper.

3. Grill skewers for 5-7 minutes per side until chicken is cooked through and vegetables are tender.

4. Cook couscous in chicken broth according to package instructions.

5. Serve skewers with a side of couscous and tzatziki sauce.

Nutritional Facts (Per Serving): Calories: 600 | Sugars: 6g | Fat: 20g | Carbohydrates: 50g | Protein: 50g | Fiber: 5g | Sodium: 800mg

Balsamic Glazed Steak Tips

Prep: 15 mins | Cook: 25 mins | Serves: 4

Ingredients:

- 1.5 lbs steak tips (680g)
- 1/4 cup balsamic vinegar (60ml)
- 2 tbsp soy sauce (30ml)
- 2 tbsp olive oil (30ml)
- 2 cloves garlic, minced (10g)
- 1 tbsp brown sugar (15g)
- 2 lbs baby potatoes, halved (900g)
- 1 tbsp fresh rosemary, chopped (5g)
- 1 lb asparagus, trimmed (450g)
- Salt and pepper to taste

Instructions:

1. In a bowl, mix balsamic vinegar, soy sauce, olive oil, minced garlic, and brown sugar. Marinate steak tips for at least 30 minutes.
2. Preheat oven to 400°F (200°C). Toss baby potatoes with olive oil, chopped rosemary, salt, and pepper. Roast for 20-25 minutes until tender.
3. Preheat grill to medium-high heat. Grill steak tips for 4-5 minutes per side until desired doneness.
4. Toss asparagus with olive oil, salt, and pepper. Grill for 5-7 minutes until tender.
5. Serve steak tips with roasted potatoes and grilled asparagus.

Nutritional Facts (Per Serving): Calories: 600 | Sugars: 8g | Fat: 25g | Carbohydrates: 50g | Protein: 40g | Fiber: 6g | Sodium: 700mg

Teriyaki Chicken Legs

Prep: 15 mins | Cook: 30 mins | Serves: 4

Ingredients:

- 8 chicken thighs (2 lbs) (900g)
- 1/2 cup teriyaki sauce (120ml)
- 2 cups jasmine rice (370g)
- 4 cups water (960ml)
- 2 tbsp vegetable oil (30ml)
- 1 bell pepper, sliced (150g)
- 1 cup broccoli florets (150g)
- 1 carrot, julienned (50g)
- 2 cloves garlic, minced (10g)
- Salt and pepper to taste

Instructions:

1. Preheat grill to medium-high heat. Brush chicken thighs with teriyaki sauce. Grill for 6-8 minutes per side until fully cooked.
2. Cook jasmine rice in water according to package instructions.
3. In a large skillet, heat vegetable oil over medium-high heat. Add garlic, bell pepper, broccoli, and carrot. Stir-fry until vegetables are tender, about 5-7 minutes. Season with salt and pepper.
4. Serve teriyaki chicken thighs with jasmine rice and stir-fried vegetables.

Nutritional Facts (Per Serving): Calories: 600 | Sugars: 10g | Fat: 25g | Carbohydrates: 55g | Protein: 35g | Fiber: 4g | Sodium: 800mg

CHAPTER 11: APPETIZERS

Cheesy Grilled Potatoes

Prep: 10 mins | Cook: 20 mins | Serves: 4

Ingredients:

- 1 lb russet potatoes, sliced (450g)
- 2 tbsp olive oil (30ml)
- 1 cup shredded cheddar cheese (120g)
- 2 tbsp chopped fresh parsley (8g)
- Salt and pepper to taste

Instructions:

1. Preheat grill to medium-high heat.
2. Toss potato slices in olive oil, salt, and pepper.
3. Grill potatoes for 15 minutes, flipping halfway, until tender.
4. Sprinkle cheese over potatoes and grill for another 2-3 minutes until cheese melts.
5. Garnish with chopped parsley before serving.

Nutritional Facts (Per Serving): Calories: 400 | Sugars: 1g | Fat: 22g | Carbohydrates: 35g | Protein: 12g | Fiber: 3g | Sodium: 400mg

Corn Fritters with Jalapeño

Prep: 5 mins | Cook: 15 mins | Serves: 4

Ingredients:

- 2 cups corn kernels (300g)
- 1 jalapeño, finely chopped
- 1/2 cup all-purpose flour (60g)
- 1/4 cup cornmeal (30g)
- 2 large eggs, beaten
- 1/4 cup milk (60ml)
- 1/4 cup chopped fresh cilantro (10g)
- 1/2 tsp baking powder (2g)
- 1/2 tsp salt (2g)
- 1/4 cup olive oil (60ml) for frying

Instructions:

1. In a large bowl, combine corn, jalapeño, flour, cornmeal, baking powder, and salt.
2. Add beaten eggs, milk, and cilantro to the mixture, stirring until well combined.
3. Heat olive oil in a skillet over medium heat.
4. Drop spoonfuls of batter into the skillet, flattening slightly with a spatula.
5. Cook fritters for 3-4 minutes per side until golden brown and crispy.
6. Drain on paper towels and serve hot.

Nutritional Facts (Per Serving): Calories: 400 | Sugars: 3g | Fat: 20g | Carbohydrates: 45g | Protein: 9g | Fiber: 4g | Sodium: 400mg

Garlic Parmesan Grilled Asparagus

Prep: 10 mins | Cook: 10 mins | Serves: 2

Ingredients:

- 1 lb asparagus, trimmed (450g)
- 2 tbsp olive oil (30ml)
- 1/4 cup grated Parmesan cheese (25g)
- 2 cloves garlic, minced (6g)
- Salt and pepper to taste

Instructions:

1. Preheat grill to medium-high heat.
2. Toss asparagus with olive oil, garlic, salt, and pepper.
3. Grill asparagus for 5-7 minutes, turning occasionally, until tender and slightly charred.
4. Sprinkle with Parmesan cheese and grill for an additional 1-2 minutes until cheese melts.

Nutritional Facts (Per Serving): Calories: 400 | Sugars: 2g | Fat: 30g | Carbohydrates: 18g | Protein: 14g | Fiber: 8g | Sodium: 400mg

Crispy Chicken Tenders

Prep: 15 mins | Cook: 15 mins | Serves: 2

Ingredients:

- 1 lb chicken tenders (450g)
- 1 cup all-purpose flour (120g)
- 2 large eggs, beaten
- 1 cup breadcrumbs (120g)
- 1/2 cup grated Parmesan cheese (50g)
- 1 tsp garlic powder (5g)
- 1 tsp paprika (5g)
- 1/2 tsp salt (2g)
- 1/4 tsp black pepper (1g)
- 1/4 cup olive oil (60ml) for frying
- 1/2 cup low carb sweetener (120ml) for dipping sauce

Instructions:

1. In a shallow dish, combine flour, garlic powder, paprika, salt, and pepper.
2. In another dish, beat eggs.
3. In a third dish, combine breadcrumbs and Parmesan cheese.
4. Dredge each chicken tender in the flour mixture, then dip in beaten eggs, and finally coat with breadcrumb mixture.
5. Heat olive oil in a large skillet over medium heat.
6. Fry chicken tenders for 3-4 minutes per side until golden brown and cooked through.
7. Serve with a tangy dipping sauce.

Nutritional Facts (Per Serving): Calories: 400 | Sugars: 2g | Fat: 22g | Carbohydrates: 20g | Protein: 30g | Fiber: 1g | Sodium: 400mg

Buffalo Cauliflower Bites

Prep: 15 mins | Cook: 25 mins | Serves: 2

Ingredients:

- 1 medium head of cauliflower, cut into florets (600g)
- 1/2 cup all-purpose flour (60g)
- 1/2 cup water (120ml)
- 1 tsp garlic powder (5g)
- 1/2 tsp paprika (2.5g)
- 1/2 tsp salt (2.5g)
- 1/4 cup buffalo sauce (60ml)
- 1/4 cup ranch dressing (60ml) for serving

Instructions:

1. Preheat oven to 450°F (230°C).
2. In a bowl, mix flour, water, garlic powder, paprika, and salt to form a batter.
3. Dip cauliflower florets in the batter, shaking off excess.
4. Place on a baking sheet lined with parchment paper.
5. Bake for 20 minutes, flipping halfway through.
6. Toss baked cauliflower in buffalo sauce.
7. Return to oven and bake for an additional 5 minutes.
8. Serve with ranch dressing.

Nutritional Facts (Per Serving): Calories: 400 | Sugars: 4g | Fat: 18g | Carbohydrates: 50g | Protein: 8g | Fiber: 8g | Sodium: 800mg

Baked Jalapeño Poppers

Prep: 15 mins | Cook: 20 mins | Serves: 2

Ingredients:

- 6 large jalapeño peppers, halved and seeded (100g)
- 4 oz cream cheese, softened (115g)
- 1/2 cup shredded cheddar cheese (60g)
- 1/2 tsp garlic powder (2.5g)
- 1/2 tsp onion powder (2.5g)
- 6 slices bacon, cut in half (100g)

Instructions:

1. Preheat oven to 400°F (200°C).
2. In a bowl, mix cream cheese, cheddar cheese, garlic powder, and onion powder.
3. Fill each jalapeño half with the cheese mixture.
4. Wrap each stuffed jalapeño with half a slice of bacon, securing with a toothpick.
5. Place on a baking sheet lined with parchment paper.
6. Bake for 15-20 minutes until bacon is crispy.

Nutritional Facts (Per Serving): Calories: 400 | Sugars: 3g | Fat: 35g | Carbohydrates: 5g | Protein:10g | Fiber: 2g | Sodium: 700mg

Spinach and Artichoke Dip Cups

Prep: 15 mins | Cook: 20 mins | Serves: 2

Ingredients:

- 12 wonton wrappers (90g)
- 1 cup chopped spinach (30g)
- 1/2 cup chopped artichoke hearts (75g)
- 4 oz cream cheese, softened (115g)
- 1/4 cup grated Parmesan cheese (25g)
- 1/4 cup shredded mozzarella cheese (30g)
- 1/4 cup sour cream (60g)
- 1 garlic clove, minced (3g)
- 1/2 tsp salt (2.5g)
- 1/4 tsp black pepper (1g)

Instructions:

1. Preheat oven to 375°F (190°C).
2. Place wonton wrappers in a mini muffin tin, pressing down to form cups.
3. In a bowl, mix spinach, artichoke hearts, cream cheese, Parmesan cheese, mozzarella cheese, sour cream, garlic, salt, and pepper.
4. Spoon the mixture into the wonton cups.
5. Bake for 15-20 minutes until golden and bubbly.

Nutritional Facts (Per Serving): Calories: 400 | Sugars: 2g | Fat: 25g | Carbohydrates: 30g | Protein: 10g | Fiber: 3g | Sodium: 800mg

Mini Meatballs

Prep: 10 mins | Cook: 15 mins | Serves: 2

Ingredients:

- 1/2 lb ground beef (225g)
- 1/4 cup breadcrumbs (30g)
- 1/4 cup grated Parmesan cheese (25g)
- 1 large egg, beaten
- 1 garlic clove, minced (3g)
- 1 tsp Italian seasoning (5g)
- 1/2 tsp salt (2.5g)
- 1/4 tsp black pepper (1g)
- 1 cup marinara sauce (240ml)

Instructions:

1. Preheat oven to 400°F (200°C).
2. In a bowl, mix ground beef, breadcrumbs, Parmesan cheese, egg, garlic, Italian seasoning, salt, and pepper.
3. Roll mixture into bite-sized meatballs and place on a baking sheet lined with parchment paper.
4. Bake for 12-15 minutes until cooked through.
5. Serve with marinara sauce.

Nutritional Facts (Per Serving): Calories: 400 | Sugars: 5g | Fat: 25g | Carbohydrates: 15g | Protein: 25g | Fiber: 2g | Sodium: 900mg

CHAPTER 12: APPETIZING DIPS AND SPREADS

Classic Hummus

Prep: 10 mins | Cook: None | Serves: 2

Ingredients:

- 1 can chickpeas, drained and rinsed (15 oz / 425g)
- 1/4 cup fresh lemon juice (60ml)
- 1/4 cup well-stirred tahini (60g)
- 1 small garlic clove, minced (3g)
- 2 tbsp olive oil (30ml)
- 1/2 tsp ground cumin (2.5g)
- Salt to taste
- 2-3 tbsp water (30-45ml)
- Paprika for garnish
- Pita chips and fresh vegetables for serving

Instructions:

1. In a food processor, combine chickpeas, lemon juice, tahini, garlic, olive oil, cumin, and salt.
2. Process until smooth, adding water as needed to achieve desired consistency.
3. Transfer to a serving bowl, drizzle with additional olive oil, and sprinkle with paprika.
4. Serve with pita chips and fresh vegetables.

Nutritional Facts (Per Serving): Calories: 400 | Sugars: 2g | Fat: 18g | Carbohydrates: 44g | Protein: 12g | Fiber: 10g | Sodium: 400mg

Spinach and Artichoke Dip

Prep: 10 mins | Cook: 20 mins | Serves: 2

Ingredients:

- 1 cup chopped spinach (30g)
- 1 cup chopped artichoke hearts (120g)
- 4 oz cream cheese, softened (115g)
- 1/4 cup sour cream (60g)
- 1/4 cup Greek yogurt (60g)
- 1/2 cup grated Parmesan cheese (50g)
- 1/2 cup shredded mozzarella cheese (60g)
- 1 garlic clove, minced (3g)
- Salt and pepper to taste
- Toasted baguette slices for serving

Instructions:

1. Preheat oven to 375°F (190°C).
2. In a bowl, mix spinach, artichoke hearts, cream cheese, sour cream, Greek yogurt, Parmesan cheese, mozzarella cheese, garlic, salt, and pepper.
3. Transfer mixture to a baking dish.
4. Bake for 20 minutes until bubbly and golden.
5. Serve warm with toasted baguette slices.

Nutritional Facts (Per Serving): Calories: 400 | Sugars: 2g | Fat: 32g | Carbohydrates: 12g | Protein: 10g | Fiber: 4g | Sodium: 800mg

Guacamole

Prep: 10 mins | Cook: None | Serves: 2

Ingredients:

- 2 ripe avocados, peeled and pitted (400g)
- 1 lime, juiced (50ml)
- 1/2 cup diced tomatoes (75g)
- 1/4 cup chopped cilantro (15g)
- 1/4 cup finely chopped red onion (40g)
- 1 garlic clove, minced (3g)
- Salt to taste
- Tortilla chips for serving

Instructions:

1. In a bowl, mash avocados with lime juice until smooth.
2. Stir in tomatoes, cilantro, red onion, garlic, and salt.
3. Serve immediately with tortilla chips.

Nutritional Facts (Per Serving): Calories: 400 | Sugars: 2g | Fat: 35g | Carbohydrates: 18g | Protein: 5g | Fiber: 12g | Sodium: 400mg

Buffalo Chicken Dip

Prep: 10 mins | Cook: 20 mins | Serves: 2

Ingredients:

- 1 cup shredded cooked chicken (150g)
- 1/4 cup hot sauce (60ml)
- 4 oz cream cheese, softened (115g)
- 1/2 cup shredded cheddar cheese (60g)
- 1/4 cup sour cream (60g)
- 1/4 cup chopped green onions (25g)
- Celery sticks for serving

Instructions:

1. Preheat oven to 375°F (190°C).
2. In a bowl, mix chicken, hot sauce, cream cheese, cheddar cheese, sour cream, and green onions.
3. Transfer mixture to a baking dish.
4. Bake for 20 minutes until bubbly and golden.
5. Serve warm with celery sticks.

Nutritional Facts (Per Serving): Calories: 400 | Sugars: 2g | Fat: 30g | Carbohydrates: 5g | Protein: 25g | Fiber: 1g | Sodium: 800mg

Tzatziki Sauce

Prep: 10 mins | Cook: None | Serves: 2

Ingredients:

- 1 cup Greek yogurt (240ml)
- 1/2 cucumber, grated and drained (100g)
- 1 tbsp olive oil (15ml)
- 1 tbsp lemon juice (15ml)
- 1 garlic clove, minced (3g)
- 1 tbsp chopped fresh dill (5g)
- Salt to taste
- Pita bread for serving

Instructions:

1. In a bowl, combine Greek yogurt, grated cucumber, olive oil, lemon juice, garlic, dill, and salt.
2. Mix well until smooth.
3. Serve chilled with pita bread.

Nutritional Facts (Per Serving): Calories: 400 | Sugars: 6g | Fat: 20g | Carbohydrates: 35g | Protein: 12g | Fiber: 3g | Sodium: 400mg

Queso Dip

Prep: 10 mins | Cook: 10 mins | Serves: 2

Ingredients:

- 1 cup shredded cheddar cheese (120g)
- 1/2 cup milk (120ml)
- 1/2 cup diced tomatoes with green chilies, drained (120g)
- 1 tbsp butter (15g)
- 1 tbsp all-purpose flour (8g)
- 1/4 tsp garlic powder (1g)
- 1/4 tsp onion powder (1g)
- Salt to taste
- Tortilla chips for serving

Instructions:

1. In a saucepan over medium heat, melt butter and stir in flour. Cook for 1 minute.
2. Gradually whisk in milk until smooth and slightly thickened.
3. Add shredded cheddar cheese, stirring until melted.
4. Stir in diced tomatoes with green chilies, garlic powder, onion powder, and salt.
5. Serve warm with tortilla chips.

Nutritional Facts (Per Serving): Calories: 400 | Sugars: 4g | Fat: 28g | Carbohydrates: 20g | Protein: 12g | Fiber: 2g | Sodium: 800mg

CHAPTER 13: DESSERTS: Desserts On The Griddle

Grilled Pineapple with Honey and Cinnamon

Prep: 10 mins | Cook: 10 mins | Serves: 2

Ingredients:

- 1 pineapple, peeled, cored, and sliced (500g)
- 2 tbsp honey (30ml)
- 1 tsp ground cinnamon (5g)

Instructions:

1. Preheat grill to medium-high heat.
2. Grill pineapple slices for 3-4 minutes per side until grill marks appear.
3. Drizzle honey over grilled pineapple and sprinkle with cinnamon.

Nutritional Facts (Per Serving): Calories: 400 | Sugars: 72g | Fat: 0g | Carbohydrates: 105g | Protein: 2g | Fiber: 12g | Sodium: 5mg

Chocolate Banana Quesadillas

Prep: 5 mins | Cook: 5 mins | Serves: 2

Ingredients:

- 2 large flour tortillas (120g)
- 1/2 cup chocolate chips (90g)
- 1 large banana, sliced (120g)
- 1 tbsp butter (15g)

Instructions:

1. Preheat a skillet over medium heat.
2. Spread chocolate chips evenly over one tortilla.
3. Arrange banana slices over the chocolate and top with the second tortilla.
4. Melt butter in the skillet and cook the quesadilla for 2-3 minutes per side until golden brown and the chocolate is melted.
5. Slice into wedges and serve warm.

Nutritional Facts (Per Serving): Calories: 400 | Sugars: 24g | Fat: 20g | Carbohydrates: 52g | Protein: 6g | Fiber: 4g | Sodium: 200mg

Cinnamon Sugar Grilled Donuts

Prep: 5 mins | Cook: 5 mins | Serves: 2

Ingredients:

- 4 plain donuts (240g)
- 2 tbsp melted butter (30g)
- 1/4 cup granulated sugar (50g)
- 1 tsp ground cinnamon (5g)

Instructions:

1. Preheat grill to medium heat.
2. Brush both sides of the donuts with melted butter.
3. Grill donuts for 1-2 minutes per side until grill marks appear.
4. Mix sugar and cinnamon in a shallow dish.
5. Coat grilled donuts in the cinnamon sugar mixture.

Nutritional Facts (Per Serving): Calories: 400 | Sugars: 22g | Fat: 18g | Carbohydrates: 52g | Protein: 5g | Fiber: 1g | Sodium: 300mg

Grilled Pound Cake with Berries

Prep: 5 mins | Cook: 5 mins | Serves: 2

Ingredients:

- 4 slices pound cake (200g)
- 1 cup mixed fresh berries (150g)
- 1 tbsp butter (15g)
- 1/4 cup whipped cream (60ml)

Instructions:

1. Preheat grill to medium heat.
2. Brush pound cake slices with butter.
3. Grill pound cake for 2-3 minutes per side until lightly toasted.
4. Top with mixed fresh berries and a dollop of whipped cream.

Nutritional Facts (Per Serving): Calories: 400 | Sugars: 24g | Fat: 20g | Carbohydrates: 52g | Protein: 5g | Fiber: 4g | Sodium: 200mg

Griddled Chocolate Chip Cookies

Prep: 10 mins | Cook: 10 mins | Serves: 2

Ingredients:

- 1/2 cup all-purpose flour (60g)
- 1/4 tsp baking soda (1g)
- 1/8 tsp salt (0.5g)
- 1/4 cup unsalted butter, softened (60g)
- 1/4 cup brown sugar (50g)
- 1/4 cup granulated sugar (50g)
- 1/2 tsp vanilla extract (2.5ml)
- 1 small egg (30g)
- 1/2 cup chocolate chips (90g)

Instructions:

1. Preheat griddle to medium heat.
2. In a bowl, whisk together flour, baking soda, and salt.
3. In another bowl, cream butter, brown sugar, and granulated sugar until fluffy.
4. Beat in vanilla extract and egg.
5. Gradually mix in dry ingredients.
6. Fold in chocolate chips.
7. Drop spoonfuls of dough onto the griddle, flattening slightly.
8. Cook for 2-3 minutes per side until golden brown.

Nutritional Facts (Per Serving): Calories: 400 | Sugars: 30g | Fat: 20g | Carbohydrates: 52g | Protein: 5g | Fiber: 2g | Sodium: 200mg

Grilled Strawberry Shortcake

Prep: 10 mins | Cook: 5 mins | Serves: 2

Ingredients:

- 2 shortcake biscuits (100g)
- 1 cup sliced strawberries (150g)
- 2 tbsp granulated sugar (30g)
- 1 tbsp butter (15g)
- 1/2 cup whipped cream (120ml)

Instructions:

1. Preheat grill to medium heat.
2. Toss sliced strawberries with granulated sugar.
3. Brush shortcake biscuits with butter.
4. Grill biscuits for 2-3 minutes per side until toasted.
5. Top grilled biscuits with strawberries and whipped cream.

Nutritional Facts (Per Serving): Calories: 400 | Sugars: 24g | Fat: 20g | Carbohydrates: 50g | Protein: 5g | Fiber: 3g | Sodium: 300mg

Grilled Fig and Honey Flatbread

Prep: 10 mins | Cook: 10 mins | Serves: 2

Ingredients:

- 2 flatbreads (200g)
- 6 fresh figs, halved (180g)
- 2 tbsp honey (30ml)
- 1/4 cup crumbled goat cheese (50g)
- 1 tbsp olive oil (15ml)
- 1 tbsp chopped fresh rosemary (5g)
- Salt and pepper to taste

Instructions:

1. Preheat grill to medium heat.
2. Brush figs with olive oil and grill for 2-3 minutes per side.
3. Brush flatbreads with olive oil and grill for 1-2 minutes per side until lightly toasted.
4. Top flatbreads with grilled figs, goat cheese, and rosemary.
5. Drizzle with honey and season with salt and pepper.

Nutritional Facts (Per Serving): Calories: 400 | Sugars: 22g | Fat: 18g | Carbohydrates: 52g | Protein: 8g | Fiber: 4g | Sodium: 300mg

Grilled Lemon Bars

Prep: 15 mins | Cook: 20 mins | Serves: 2

Ingredients:

- 1 cup all-purpose flour (120g)
- 1/4 cup powdered sugar (30g)
- 1/2 cup unsalted butter, softened (115g)
- 2 large eggs (100g)
- 1 cup granulated sugar (200g)
- 1/4 cup lemon juice (60ml)
- 1 tbsp lemon zest (6g)
- 1/2 tsp baking powder (2g)
- 1/4 tsp salt (1g)

Instructions:

1. Preheat grill to medium heat.
2. In a bowl, mix flour, powdered sugar, and butter until crumbly. Press into a foil-lined, greased 8x8-inch (20x20cm) baking pan.
3. Grill crust for 10 minutes until lightly golden.
4. In another bowl, whisk eggs, granulated sugar, lemon juice, lemon zest, baking powder, and salt until smooth.
5. Pour lemon mixture over the grilled crust.
6. Grill for another 10 minutes until set.
7. Cool completely before cutting into bars.

Nutritional Facts (Per Serving): Calories: 400 | Sugars: 34g | Fat: 18g | Carbohydrates: 52g | Protein: 4g | Fiber: 1g | Sodium: 200mg

CHAPTER 14: DESSERTS: Desserts for Special Occasions

Grilled Cherry Hand Pies

Prep: 15 mins | Cook: 10 mins | Serves: 2

Ingredients:

- 1 cup cherry pie filling (250g)
- 1 package refrigerated pie crusts (250g)
- 1 tbsp butter, melted (15g)
- 1 tbsp powdered sugar (15g)

Instructions:

1. Preheat grill to medium heat.
2. Roll out pie crusts and cut into 4-inch (10cm) circles.
3. Place a spoonful of cherry pie filling in the center of each circle.
4. Fold the dough over and crimp edges with a fork to seal. Brush with melted butter.
5. Grill hand pies for 4-5 minutes per side until golden brown.
6. Sprinkle with powdered sugar before serving.

Nutritional Facts (Per Serving): Calories: 400 | Sugars: 20g | Fat: 18g | Carbohydrates: 54g | Protein: 4g | Fiber: 2g | Sodium: 300mg

Grilled Strawberry Cheesecake

Prep: 15 mins | Cook: 20 mins | Serves: 2

Ingredients:

- 1 ready-made graham cracker crust (150g)
- 1 cup cream cheese, softened (240g)
- 1/4 cup granulated sugar (50g)
- 1 large egg (50g)
- 1 tsp vanilla extract (5ml)
- 1 cup sliced strawberries (150g)
- 2 tbsp chocolate sauce (30ml)

Instructions:

1. Preheat grill to medium heat.
2. In a bowl, mix cream cheese, sugar, egg, and vanilla extract until smooth.
3. Pour mixture into graham cracker crust.
4. Grill cheesecake for 15-20 minutes until set.
5. Let cool slightly, then top with sliced strawberries and drizzle with chocolate sauce.

Nutritional Facts (Per Serving): Calories: 400 | Sugars: 26g | Fat: 24g | Carbohydrates: 40g | Protein: 6g | Fiber: 2g | Sodium: 300mg

Lemon Ricotta Griddle Cake

Prep: 10 mins | Cook: 10 mins | Serves: 2

Ingredients:

- 1 cup ricotta cheese (240g)
- 1/2 cup all-purpose flour (60g)
- 1/4 cup granulated sugar (50g)
- 2 large eggs (100g)
- Zest of 1 lemon (6g)
- 1 tbsp lemon juice (15ml)
- 1/2 tsp baking powder (2g)
- 1/4 tsp salt (1g)
- 1 tbsp butter (15g)
- Powdered sugar for topping (15g)

Instructions:

1. In a bowl, mix ricotta cheese, flour, sugar, eggs, lemon zest, lemon juice, baking powder, and salt until smooth.
2. Preheat griddle to medium heat and melt butter.
3. Pour batter onto the griddle to form cakes, about 1/4 cup (60ml) each.
4. Cook for 2-3 minutes per side until golden brown and cooked through.
5. Top with powdered sugar and serve warm.

Nutritional Facts (Per Serving): Calories: 400 | Sugars: 20g | Fat: 20g | Carbohydrates: 40g | Protein: 15g | Fiber: 1g | Sodium: 300mg

Grilled Tiramisu

Prep: 15 mins | Cook: 10 mins | Serves: 2

Ingredients:

- 4 slices sponge cake (200g)
- 1 cup mascarpone cheese (240g)
- 1/4 cup granulated sugar (50g)
- 1/4 cup strong brewed espresso, cooled (60ml)
- 1 tbsp cocoa powder (15g)
- 1 tbsp coffee liqueur (optional) (15ml)
- 1 tsp vanilla extract (5ml)

Instructions:

1. Preheat grill to medium heat.
2. Grill sponge cake slices for 1-2 minutes per side until lightly toasted.
3. In a bowl, mix mascarpone cheese, sugar, vanilla extract, and coffee liqueur until smooth.
4. Layer grilled sponge cake, mascarpone mixture, and drizzle with espresso in serving glasses.
5. Dust with cocoa powder.

Nutritional Facts (Per Serving): Calories: 400 | Sugars: 24g | Fat: 25g | Carbohydrates: 34g | Protein: 6g | Fiber: 1g | Sodium: 200mg

Grilled Apple Pie

Prep: 15 mins | Cook: 10 mins | Serves: 2

Ingredients:

- 2 cups apple pie filling (500g)
- 1 package refrigerated pie crusts (250g)
- 1 tbsp butter, melted (15g)
- 1 tbsp granulated sugar (15g)
- 1 tsp ground cinnamon (5g)

Instructions:

1. Preheat grill to medium heat.
2. Roll out pie crusts and cut into 4-inch (10cm) circles.
3. Place a spoonful of apple pie filling in the center of each circle.
4. Fold the dough over and crimp edges with a fork to seal.
5. Brush with melted butter and sprinkle with sugar and cinnamon.
6. Grill hand pies for 4-5 minutes per side until golden brown.

Nutritional Facts (Per Serving): Calories: 400 | Sugars: 20g | Fat: 18g | Carbohydrates: 54g | Protein: 4g | Fiber: 3g | Sodium: 300mg

Pecan Pie Griddle Bars

Prep: 15 mins | Cook: 15 mins | Serves: 2

Ingredients:

- 1 cup all-purpose flour (120g)
- 1/4 cup powdered sugar (30g)
- 1/2 cup unsalted butter, softened (115g)
- 1 cup chopped pecans (125g)
- 1/2 cup granulated sugar (100g)
- 1/2 cup corn syrup (120ml)
- 2 large eggs (100g)
- 1 tsp vanilla extract (5ml)
- 1/4 tsp salt (1g)

Instructions:

1. Preheat griddle to medium heat.
2. In a bowl, mix flour, powdered sugar, and butter until crumbly. Press into a foil-lined, greased 8x8-inch (20x20cm) baking pan.
3. Grill crust for 10 minutes until lightly golden.
4. In another bowl, whisk pecans, granulated sugar, corn syrup, eggs, vanilla extract, and salt until smooth.
5. Pour pecan mixture over the grilled crust.
6. Grill for another 10 minutes until set.
7. Cool completely before cutting into bars.

Nutritional Facts (Per Serving): Calories: 400 | Sugars: 28g | Fat: 24g | Carbohydrates: 40g | Protein: 4g | Fiber: 2g | Sodium: 200mg

CHAPTER 15: DINNER: Low Fat & Low CalorieOptions

Grilled Lemon Herb Chicken Breast

Prep: 15 mins | Cook: 20 mins | Serves: 2

Ingredients:

- 2 boneless, skinless chicken breasts (250g each)
- 2 tbsp olive oil (30ml)
- Juice and zest of 1 lemon
- 1 tsp dried oregano (1g)
- 1 tsp dried thyme (1g)
- 1/2 tsp garlic powder (1g)
- Salt and pepper to taste
- 2 cups steamed broccoli (300g)

Instructions:

1. Marinate chicken breasts in olive oil, lemon juice, lemon zest, oregano, thyme, garlic powder, salt, and pepper for at least 10 minutes.
2. Preheat grill to medium-high heat.
3. Grill chicken breasts for 6-7 minutes per side or until fully cooked.
4. Serve with steamed broccoli on the side.

Nutritional Facts (Per Serving): Calories: 400 | Sugars: 2g | Fat: 16g | Carbohydrates: 12g | Protein: 52g | Fiber: 6g | Sodium: 400mg

Herb-Crusted Grilled Tilapia

Prep: 15 mins | Cook: 15 mins | Serves: 2

Ingredients:

- 2 tilapia fillets (200g each)
- 2 tbsp olive oil (30ml)
- 1/4 cup breadcrumbs (30g)
- 1 tbsp dried mixed herbs (thyme, rosemary, oregano) (5g)
- 1 tsp garlic powder (1g)
- Salt and pepper to taste
- 4 cups fresh spinach (250g)
- 1 clove garlic, minced
- 1 tbsp olive oil (15ml) (for sautéing spinach)

Instructions:

1. Brush tilapia fillets with olive oil.
2. In a bowl, mix breadcrumbs, dried herbs, garlic powder, salt, and pepper.
3. Coat the fillets with the breadcrumb mixture.
4. Preheat grill to medium-high heat.
5. Grill tilapia for 4-5 minutes per side until cooked through.
6. In a skillet, sauté spinach with minced garlic in olive oil until wilted, about 3-4 minutes.
7. Serve the tilapia with sautéed spinach.

Nutritional Facts (Per Serving): Calories: 400 | Sugars: 2g | Fat: 20g | Carbohydrates: 16g | Protein: 42g | Fiber: 6g | Sodium: 350mg

Turkey and Veggie Stir-Fry

Prep: 15 mins | Cook: 15 mins | Serves: 2

Ingredients:

- 1/2 lb lean turkey strips (225g)
- 1 tbsp olive oil (15ml)
- 1 red bell pepper, sliced (150g)
- 1 cup broccoli florets (150g)
- 1 carrot, julienned (100g)
- 1 small onion, sliced (100g)
- 2 tbsp low-sodium soy sauce (30ml)
- 1 tsp grated ginger (1g)
- 1 clove garlic, minced
- 1 tsp low carb sweeteners (1g)
- 1/2 tsp sesame oil (2.5ml)
- Salt and pepper to taste

Instructions:

1. Heat olive oil in a large skillet over medium-high heat.
2. Add turkey strips, cook until browned, about 5 minutes. Remove and set aside.
3. In the same skillet, add bell pepper, broccoli, carrot, and onion. Stir-fry for 5 minutes.
4. Return turkey to the skillet, add soy sauce, ginger, garlic, low carb sweeteners, sesame oil, salt, and pepper. Stir-fry for another 5 minutes.

Nutritional Facts (Per Serving): Calories: 400 | Sugars: 5g | Fat: 14g | Carbohydrates: 20g | Protein: 40g | Fiber: 8g | Sodium: 600mg

Citrus Glazed Grilled Chicken

Prep: 15 mins | Cook: 20 mins | Serves: 2

Ingredients:

- 2 boneless, skinless chicken breasts (250g each)
- 2 tbsp olive oil (30ml)
- Juice and zest of 1 orange
- Juice and zest of 1 lemon
- 2 tbsp low carb sweeteners (30g)
- 1 tsp garlic powder (1g)
- 1 tsp onion powder (1g)
- Salt and pepper to taste
- 1 bunch asparagus, trimmed (250g)

Instructions:

1. Marinate chicken breasts in olive oil, orange juice, lemon juice, orange zest, lemon zest, low carb sweeteners, garlic powder, onion powder, salt, and pepper for 10 minutes.
2. Preheat grill to medium-high heat.
3. Grill chicken breasts for 6-7 minutes per side or until fully cooked.
4. Grill asparagus for 5-6 minutes until tender.
5. Serve the chicken with grilled asparagus.

Nutritional Facts (Per Serving): Calories: 400 | Sugars: 6g | Fat: 16g | Carbohydrates: 14g | Protein: 50g | Fiber: 6g | Sodium: 300mg

Rosemary Garlic Pork Tenderloin

Prep: 15 mins | Cook: 25 mins | Serves: 2

Ingredients:

- 1 lb pork tenderloin (450g)
- 2 tbsp olive oil (30ml)
- 2 cloves garlic, minced
- 2 tsp dried rosemary (4g)
- Salt and pepper to taste
- 2 cups Brussels sprouts, halved (300g)

Instructions:

1. Marinate pork tenderloin with olive oil, minced garlic, rosemary, salt, and pepper for 10 minutes.
2. Preheat grill to medium-high heat.
3. Grill pork tenderloin for 12-15 minutes per side or until internal temperature reaches 145°F (63°C).
4. Roast Brussels sprouts in a preheated oven at 400°F (200°C) for 20 minutes.
5. Serve the pork tenderloin with roasted Brussels sprouts.

Nutritional Facts (Per Serving): Calories: 400 | Sugars: 4g | Fat: 18g | Carbohydrates: 16g | Protein: 44g | Fiber: 8g | Sodium: 300mg

Grilled Shrimp and Zucchini Boats

Prep: 15 mins | Cook: 15 mins | Serves: 2

Ingredients:

- 1/2 lb shrimp, peeled and deveined (225g)
- 2 medium zucchinis, halved and hollowed (300g each)
- 1 tbsp olive oil (15ml)
- 2 cloves garlic, minced
- 1/2 cup diced tomatoes (100g)
- 2 tbsp fresh parsley, chopped (8g)
- 1 tbsp lemon juice (15ml)
- Salt and pepper to taste

Instructions:

1. Marinate shrimp with olive oil, garlic, lemon juice, salt, and pepper for 10 minutes.
2. Preheat grill to medium-high heat.
3. Stuff zucchini halves with marinated shrimp and diced tomatoes.
4. Grill zucchini boats for 8-10 minutes until shrimp are fully cooked and zucchini is tender.
5. Garnish with fresh parsley and serve.

Nutritional Facts (Per Serving): Calories: 400 | Sugars: 5g | Fat: 12g | Carbohydrates: 20g | Protein: 50g | Fiber: 8g | Sodium: 400mg

Lemon Dill Grilled Salmon

Prep: 15 mins | Cook: 20 mins | Serves: 2

Ingredients:

- 2 salmon fillets (300g each)
- 2 tbsp olive oil (30ml)
- Juice and zest of 1 lemon
- 2 tbsp fresh dill, chopped (8g)
- 1 tsp garlic powder (1g)
- Salt and pepper to taste
- 2 cups assorted roasted vegetables (carrots, bell peppers, zucchini) (400g)

Instructions:

1. Marinate salmon fillets with olive oil, lemon juice, lemon zest, dill, garlic powder, salt, and pepper for 10 minutes.
2. Preheat grill to medium-high heat.
3. Grill salmon for 4-5 minutes per side until cooked through.
4. Roast vegetables in a preheated oven at 400°F (200°C) for 20 minutes.
5. Serve salmon with a side of roasted vegetables.

Nutritional Facts (Per Serving): Calories: 400 | Sugars: 5g | Fat: 20g | Carbohydrates: 12g | Protein: 40g | Fiber: 4g | Sodium: 200mg

Grilled Chicken and Mango Salad

Prep: 15 mins | Cook: 15 mins | Serves: 2

Ingredients:

- 2 boneless, skinless chicken breasts (250g each)
- 1 tbsp olive oil (15ml)
- 1 ripe mango, sliced (200g)
- 4 cups mixed greens (120g)
- 1/4 cup red onion, thinly sliced (40g)
- 1/4 cup cucumber, sliced (50g)
- 2 tbsp low carb sweeteners (30g)
- 2 tbsp lemon juice (30ml)
- 1 tbsp olive oil (15ml) (for dressing)
- Salt and pepper to taste

Instructions:

1. Marinate chicken breasts with olive oil, salt, and pepper for 10 minutes.
2. Preheat grill to medium-high heat.
3. Grill chicken for 6-7 minutes per side until fully cooked.
4. In a large bowl, combine mixed greens, mango slices, red onion, and cucumber.
5. In a small bowl, whisk together lemon juice, olive oil, low carb sweeteners, salt, and pepper for the dressing.
6. Slice the grilled chicken and arrange on top of the salad.
7. Drizzle with the dressing and serve.

Nutritional Facts (Per Serving): Calories: 400 | Sugars: 10g | Fat: 18g | Carbohydrates: 20g | Protein: 36g | Fiber: 4g | Sodium: 250mg

Grilled Pineapple Chicken with Grilled Eggplant and Tomato Salad

Prep: 15 mins | Cook: 20 mins | Serves: 2

Ingredients:

- 2 boneless, skinless chicken breasts (250g each)
- 1 tbsp olive oil (15ml)
- Salt and pepper to taste
- 4 slices fresh pineapple (200g)
- 1 medium eggplant, sliced (300g)
- 1 tbsp olive oil (15ml) (for eggplant)
- 4 cups mixed greens (120g)
- 1 cup cherry tomatoes, halved (150g)
- 2 tbsp balsamic vinegar (30ml)
- 1 tbsp olive oil (15ml) (for dressing)

Instructions:

1. Preheat grill to medium-high.
2. Brush chicken and pineapple with olive oil, season with salt and pepper.
3. Grill chicken for 6-7 minutes per side; grill pineapple for 2-3 minutes per side.
4. Brush eggplant with olive oil, season, and grill for 3-4 minutes per side.
5. Combine mixed greens and cherry tomatoes. Top salad with grilled eggplant.
6. Whisk balsamic vinegar and olive oil, drizzle over salad.
7. Serve chicken topped with pineapple, alongside eggplant salad.

Nutritional Facts (Per Serving): Calories: 400 | Sugars: 12g | Fat: 18g | Carbohydrates: 32g | Protein: 32g | Fiber: 8g | Sodium: 250mg

Grilled Steak and Veggie Salad

Prep: 15 mins | Cook: 15 mins | Serves: 2

Ingredients:

- 1 lb flank steak (450g)
- 1 tbsp olive oil (15ml)
- Salt and pepper to taste
- 4 cups arugula (120g)
- 1 cup cherry tomatoes, halved (150g)
- 2 tbsp balsamic glaze (30ml)

Instructions:

1. Marinate flank steak with olive oil, salt, and pepper for 10 minutes.
2. Preheat grill to medium-high heat.
3. Grill steak for 5-7 minutes per side, let rest for 5 minutes, then slice thinly.
4. In a large bowl, combine arugula and cherry tomatoes.
5. Arrange steak slices on top of the salad and drizzle with balsamic glaze.

Nutritional Facts (Per Serving): Calories: 400 | Sugars: 6g | Fat: 20g | Carbohydrates: 12g | Protein: 38g | Fiber: 4g | Sodium: 250mg

CHAPTER 16: DINNER: Grilled Vegetables and Greens

Grilled Zucchini Noodles with Pesto

Prep: 15 mins | Cook: 10 mins | Serves: 2

Ingredients:

- 4 medium zucchinis, spiralized (400g)
- 2 tbsp olive oil (30ml)
- 1/4 cup pesto sauce (60g)
- Salt and pepper to taste
- 2 tbsp grated Parmesan cheese (10g)
- 1 tbsp pine nuts, toasted (8g)

Instructions:

1. Preheat grill to medium-high heat.
2. Toss zucchini noodles with olive oil, salt, and pepper.
3. Grill zucchini noodles in a grill basket for 3-4 minutes, tossing occasionally until tender.
4. In a bowl, toss grilled zucchini noodles with pesto sauce.
5. Top with grated Parmesan cheese and toasted pine nuts.

Nutritional Facts (Per Serving): Calories: 400 | Sugars: 6g | Fat: 32g | Carbohydrates: 20g | Protein: 10g | Fiber: 6g | Sodium: 300mg

Grilled Cauliflower Steaks

Prep: 15 mins | Cook: 20 mins | Serves: 2

Ingredients:

- 1 large cauliflower, sliced into thick steaks (600g)
- 2 tbsp olive oil (30ml)
- Salt and pepper to taste
- 2 tbsp tahini (30g)
- Juice of 1 lemon
- 1 clove garlic, minced
- 2 tbsp water (30ml)
- 1 tbsp fresh parsley, chopped (4g)

Instructions:

1. Preheat grill to medium-high heat.
2. Brush cauliflower steaks with olive oil, season with salt and pepper.
3. Grill cauliflower steaks for 8-10 minutes per side until tender.
4. In a small bowl, mix tahini, lemon juice, garlic, and water to make the sauce.
5. Drizzle lemon tahini sauce over grilled cauliflower steaks and garnish with chopped parsley.

Nutritional Facts (Per Serving): Calories: 400 | Sugars: 5g | Fat: 28g | Carbohydrates: 26g | Protein: 10g | Fiber: 10g | Sodium: 200mg

Tofu and Vegetable Stir-Fry

Prep: 15 mins | Cook: 15 mins | Serves: 2

Ingredients:

- 1 block firm tofu, cubed (300g)
- 1 tbsp olive oil (15ml)
- 2 cups broccoli florets (300g)
- 1 red bell pepper, sliced (150g)
- 1 cup mushrooms, sliced (150g)
- 2 tbsp low-sodium soy sauce (30ml)
- 1 tbsp sesame oil (15ml)
- 1 tsp grated ginger (1g)
- 1 clove garlic, minced
- 1 tsp low carb sweeteners (1g)

Instructions:

1. Heat olive oil in a large skillet over medium-high heat.
2. Add tofu cubes and cook until golden brown.
3. Add broccoli, bell pepper, and mushrooms, stir-fry for 5 minutes.
4. In a small bowl, mix soy sauce, sesame oil, ginger, garlic, and low carb sweeteners.
5. Pour sauce over vegetables and tofu, stir-fry for another 3-4 minutes.

Nutritional Facts (Per Serving): Calories: 400 | Sugars: 5g | Fat: 22g | Carbohydrates: 20g | Protein: 30g | Fiber: 8g | Sodium: 400mg

Grilled Veggie Platter

Prep: 15 mins | Cook: 20 mins | Serves: 2

Ingredients:

- 2 zucchinis, sliced (300g)
- 1 red bell pepper, sliced (150g)
- 1 yellow bell pepper, sliced (150g)
- 1 cup mushrooms, halved (150g)
- 2 tbsp olive oil (30ml)
- 1 tsp dried oregano (1g)
- 1 tsp garlic powder (1g)
- Salt and pepper to taste

Instructions:

1. Preheat grill to medium-high heat.
2. Toss sliced zucchinis, bell peppers, and mushrooms with olive oil, oregano, garlic powder, salt, and pepper.
3. Grill vegetables for 4-5 minutes per side until tender and slightly charred.
4. Serve the grilled vegetables on a platter.

Nutritional Facts (Per Serving): Calories: 400 | Sugars: 8g | Fat: 18g | Carbohydrates: 42g | Protein: 10g | Fiber: 12g | Sodium: 200mg

Grilled Zucchini with Parmesan

Prep: 10 mins | Cook: 10 mins | Serves: 2

Ingredients:

- 2 medium zucchinis, sliced (300g)
- 2 tbsp olive oil (30ml)
- Salt and pepper to taste
- 1/4 cup grated Parmesan cheese (25g)

Instructions:

1. Preheat grill to medium-high heat.
2. Toss zucchini slices with olive oil, salt, and pepper.
3. Grill zucchini slices for 3-4 minutes per side until tender and grill marks appear.
4. Sprinkle grilled zucchini with Parmesan cheese before serving.

Nutritional Facts (Per Serving): Calories: 400 | Sugars: 5g | Fat: 28g | Carbohydrates: 16g | Protein: 18g | Fiber: 6g | Sodium: 350mg

Grilled Tomato and Mozzarella Salad

Prep: 10 mins | Cook: 5 mins | Serves: 2

Ingredients:

- 4 medium tomatoes, sliced (400g)
- 1 tbsp olive oil (15ml)
- Salt and pepper to taste
- 1 ball fresh mozzarella, sliced (150g)
- Fresh basil leaves for garnish
- 1 tbsp balsamic glaze (15ml)

Instructions:

1. Preheat grill to medium-high heat.
2. Brush tomato slices with olive oil and season with salt and pepper.
3. Grill tomato slices for 2-3 minutes per side until slightly charred.
4. Arrange grilled tomatoes and mozzarella slices on a plate.
5. Garnish with fresh basil leaves and drizzle with balsamic glaze before serving.

Nutritional Facts (Per Serving): Calories: 400 | Sugars: 8g | Fat: 28g | Carbohydrates: 20g | Protein: 20g | Fiber: 4g | Sodium: 300mg

CHAPTER 17: DINNER: Flavorful Seafood Dishes

Grilled Mahi Mahi with Pineapple Salsa

Prep: 15 mins | Cook: 20 mins | Serves: 2

Ingredients:

- 2 Mahi Mahi fillets (300g each)
- 2 tbsp olive oil (30ml)
- Salt and pepper to taste
- 1 cup diced pineapple (150g)
- 1/4 cup red onion, finely chopped (40g)
- 1/4 cup cilantro, chopped (15g)
- Juice of 1 lime
- 1 cup coconut rice (200g)
- 1 cup sautéed green beans (150g)

Instructions:

1. Preheat grill to medium-high heat.
2. Brush Mahi Mahi fillets with olive oil, season with salt and pepper.
3. Grill fillets for 4-5 minutes per side until cooked through.
4. In a bowl, combine pineapple, red onion, cilantro, and lime juice to make salsa.
5. Serve grilled Mahi Mahi topped with pineapple salsa, with a side of coconut rice and sautéed green beans.

Nutritional Facts (Per Serving): Calories: 400 | Sugars: 12g | Fat: 12g | Carbohydrates: 40g | Protein: 30g | Fiber: 6g | Sodium: 300mg

Grilled Tuna Steaks with Avocado

Prep: 15 mins | Cook: 20 mins | Serves: 2

Ingredients:

- 2 tuna steaks (200g each)
- 1 tbsp olive oil (15ml)
- Salt and pepper to taste
- 1 avocado, sliced (150g)
- 2 cups mixed greens (120g)
- 1 medium sweet potato, cubed and roasted (200g)
- 2 tbsp balsamic vinaigrette (30ml)

Instructions:

1. Preheat grill to medium-high heat.
2. Brush tuna steaks with olive oil, season with salt and pepper.
3. Grill tuna steaks for 2-3 minutes per side until desired doneness.
4. Arrange mixed greens on plates, top with avocado slices.

5. Serve grilled tuna steaks with roasted sweet potatoes and mixed greens salad drizzled with balsamic vinaigrette.

Nutritional Facts (Per Serving): Calories: 400 | Sugars: 6g | Fat: 20g | Carbohydrates: 30g | Protein: 28g | Fiber: 8g | Sodium: 250mg

Grilled Halibut with Mango Salsa

Prep: 15 mins | Cook: 20 mins | Serves: 2

Ingredients:

- 2 halibut fillets (300g each)
- 2 tbsp olive oil (30ml)
- Salt and pepper to taste
- 1 cup diced mango (150g)
- 1/4 cup red bell pepper, diced (40g)
- 1/4 cup red onion, finely chopped (40g)
- 2 tbsp fresh cilantro, chopped (8g)
- Juice of 1 lime
- 1 cup cooked brown rice (200g)
- 2 medium zucchinis, sliced (300g)

Instructions:

1. Preheat grill to medium-high heat.
2. Brush halibut fillets and zucchini slices with olive oil, season with salt and pepper.
3. Grill halibut fillets for 4-5 minutes per side until cooked through. Grill zucchini slices for 3-4 minutes per side until tender.
4. In a bowl, combine mango, red bell pepper, red onion, cilantro, and lime juice to make salsa.

5. Serve grilled halibut topped with mango salsa, with a side of brown rice and grilled zucchini.

Nutritional Facts (Per Serving): Calories: 400 | Sugars: 10g | Fat: 12g | Carbohydrates: 38g | Protein: 36g | Fiber: 6g | Sodium: 200mg

Grilled Swordfish with Tomato Basil Relish

Prep: 15 mins | Cook: 20 mins | Serves: 2

Ingredients:

- 2 swordfish steaks (250g each)
- 2 tbsp olive oil (30ml)
- Salt and pepper to taste
- 1 cup cherry tomatoes, halved (150g)
- 1/4 cup fresh basil, chopped (10g)
- 1 tbsp balsamic vinegar (15ml)
- 1 clove garlic, minced
- 1 cup roasted red potatoes, cubed (200g)
- 1 cup steamed green beans (150g)

Instructions:

1. Preheat grill to medium-high heat.
2. Brush swordfish steaks with olive oil, season with salt and pepper.
3. Grill swordfish steaks for 4-5 minutes per side until cooked through.
4. In a bowl, combine cherry tomatoes, basil, balsamic vinegar, and garlic to make relish.

5. Serve grilled swordfish topped with tomato basil relish, with a side of roasted red potatoes and steamed green beans.

Nutritional Facts (Per Serving): Calories: 400 | Sugars: 6g | Fat: 18g | Carbohydrates: 32g | Protein: 30g | Fiber: 6g | Sodium: 250mg

Grilled Tilapia with Garlic Lime Sauce

Prep: 15 mins | Cook: 20 mins | Serves: 2

Ingredients:

- 2 tilapia fillets (300g each)
- 2 tbsp olive oil (30ml)
- Salt and pepper to taste
- 2 cloves garlic, minced
- Juice of 1 lime
- 1 tbsp low carb sweeteners (15g)
- 1 cup cooked couscous (200g)
- 2 cups sautéed spinach (150g)

Instructions:

1. Preheat grill to medium-high heat.
2. Brush tilapia fillets with olive oil, season with salt and pepper.
3. Grill tilapia fillets for 3-4 minutes per side.
4. In a small pan, sauté minced garlic in olive oil for 1-2 minutes, then add lime juice and low carb sweeteners. Cook for another 2 minutes.
5. Serve tilapia topped with garlic lime sauce, alongside couscous and sautéed spinach.

Nutritional Facts (Per Serving): Calories: 400 | Sugars: 4g | Fat: 16g | Carbohydrates: 36g | Protein: 30g | Fiber: 4g | Sodium: 200mg

Grilled Cod with Lemon Caper Sauce

Prep: 15 mins | Cook: 20 mins | Serves: 2

Ingredients:

- 2 cod fillets (300g each)
- 2 tbsp olive oil (30ml)
- Salt and pepper to taste
- Juice of 1 lemon
- 1 tbsp capers (15g)
- 1 tbsp low carb sweeteners (15g)
- 1 cup cooked quinoa (200g)
- 2 cups roasted carrots (200g)

Instructions:

1. Preheat grill to medium-high heat.
2. Brush cod fillets with olive oil, season with salt and pepper.
3. Grill cod fillets for 4-5 minutes per side until cooked through.
4. In a small pan, combine lemon juice, capers, and low carb sweeteners. Cook for 2-3 minutes.
5. Serve cod topped with lemon caper sauce, alongside quinoa and roasted carrots.

Nutritional Facts (Per Serving): Calories: 400 | Sugars: 6g | Fat: 14g | Carbohydrates: 40g | Protein: 32g | Fiber: 6g | Sodium: 250mg

CHAPTER 18: DINNER: Family-Style Dinner Ideas

Classic BBQ Baby Back Ribs

Prep: 15 mins | Cook: 2 hours | Serves: 2

Ingredients:

- 1 rack baby back ribs (500g)
- 1 cup BBQ sauce (250ml)
- Salt and pepper to taste
- 2 cups coleslaw (300g)
- 1 cup baked beans (200g)

Instructions:

1. Preheat grill to medium heat.
2. Season ribs with salt and pepper, then brush with BBQ sauce.
3. Wrap ribs in aluminum foil and grill for 1.5 hours.
4. Remove from foil and brush with more BBQ sauce. Grill for an additional 20-30 minutes until tender and caramelized.
5. Serve ribs with coleslaw and baked beans.

Nutritional Facts (Per Serving): Calories: 400 | Sugars: 12g | Fat: 20g | Carbohydrates: 30g | Protein: 24g | Fiber: 4g | Sodium: 600mg

Honey Garlic Spare Ribs

Prep: 15 mins | Cook: 2 hours | Serves: 2

Ingredients:

- 1 rack spare ribs (500g)
- 1/4 cup honey (60ml)
- 3 cloves garlic, minced
- 2 tbsp soy sauce (30ml)
- 1 tbsp olive oil (15ml)
- Salt and pepper to taste
- 2 cups roasted sweet potatoes, cubed (400g)
- 2 cups sautéed green beans (150g)

Instructions:

1. Preheat grill to medium.
2. Mix honey, garlic, soy sauce, olive oil, salt, and pepper for the glaze.
3. Season ribs, brush with glaze, and wrap in foil. Grill ribs for 1.5 hours.
4. Unwrap, brush with more glaze, and grill for 20-30 minutes until tender and caramelized.
5. Serve with roasted sweet potatoes and sautéed green beans.

Nutritional Facts (Per Serving): Calories: 400 | Sugars: 15g | Fat: 18g | Carbohydrates: 35g | Protein: 22g | Fiber: 6g | Sodium: 400mg

Paella

Prep: 20 mins | Cook: 40 mins | Serves: 2

Ingredients:

- 1/2 cup Arborio rice (100g)
- 1 tbsp olive oil (15ml)
- 1 small onion, finely chopped (100g)
- 1 red bell pepper, diced (150g)
- 2 cloves garlic, minced
- 1/2 cup canned diced tomatoes (120g)
- 1/2 cup frozen peas (75g)
- 1/2 lb shrimp, peeled and deveined (225g)
- 1/2 lb chicken breast, diced (225g)
- 1 cup chicken broth (240ml)
- 1/4 tsp saffron threads (0.5g)
- 1 tsp smoked paprika (2g)
- Salt and pepper to taste
- Lemon wedges for garnish
- Fresh parsley, chopped (optional, for garnish)

Instructions:

1.Heat olive oil in a skillet over medium. Sauté onion and red bell pepper for 5 minutes.

2. Add garlic and tomatoes, cook for 2 minutes.

3. Stir in Arborio rice, saffron, and paprika for 1-2 minutes.

4. Add chicken broth, simmer, cover, and cook on low for 20 minutes.

5. Add shrimp, chicken, and peas, cook for 10-15 minutes until done.

6. Season with salt and pepper.

7. Garnish with lemon wedges and parsley.

Nutritional Facts (Per Serving): Calories: 400 | Sugars: 6g | Fat: 14g | Carbohydrates: 35g | Protein: 30g | Fiber: 5g | Sodium: 500mg

Grilled Sardines with Fresh Herbs

Prep: 15 mins | Cook: 20 mins | Serves: 2

Ingredients:

- 6 fresh sardines (400g)
- 2 tbsp olive oil (30ml)
- Salt and pepper to taste
- 2 tbsp fresh parsley, chopped (8g)
- 1 tbsp fresh dill, chopped (4g)
- 1 cup cooked couscous (200g)
- Juice of 1 lemon
- 2 bell peppers, sliced (300g)

Instructions:

1. Preheat grill to medium-high heat.

2. Brush sardines with olive oil, season with salt and pepper.

3. Grill sardines for 3-4 minutes per side until cooked through.

4. In a small bowl, mix parsley, dill, and lemon juice.

5. Toss cooked couscous with a bit of olive oil and lemon juice.

6. Grill bell peppers for 4-5 minutes until tender.

7. Serve grilled sardines topped with fresh herbs, with a side of lemony couscous and grilled bell peppers.

Nutritional Facts (Per Serving): Calories: 400 | Sugars: 4g | Fat: 20g | Carbohydrates: 30g | Protein: 28g | Fiber: 4g | Sodium: 300mg

Grilled Veggie Lasagna

Prep: 20 mins | Cook: 40 mins | Serves: 2

Ingredients:

- 2 medium zucchinis, sliced lengthwise (300g)
- 1 large eggplant, sliced lengthwise (400g)
- 1 cup ricotta cheese (250g)
- 1 cup marinara sauce (250g)
- 1/2 cup grated mozzarella (50g)
- 1 tbsp olive oil (15ml)
- Salt and pepper to taste
- 2 slices garlic bread (60g)

Instructions:

1. Preheat grill to medium-high heat.
2. Brush zucchini and eggplant slices with olive oil, season with salt and pepper.
3. Grill vegetables for 3-4 minutes per side until tender.
4. In a baking dish, layer grilled vegetables, ricotta, and marinara sauce. Repeat layers and top with grated mozzarella.
5. Bake in a preheated oven at 375°F (190°C) for 20 minutes until bubbly and golden.
6. Serve with garlic bread on the side.

Nutritional Facts (Per Serving): Calories: 400 | Sugars: 8g | Fat: 22g | Carbohydrates: 30g | Protein: 20g | Fiber: 6g | Sodium: 400mg

Grilled Meatloaf with Veggies

Prep: 15 mins | Cook: 40 mins | Serves: 2

Ingredients:

- 1 lb ground beef (450g)
- 1/2 cup breadcrumbs (50g)
- 1/4 cup milk (60ml)
- 1 egg (50g)
- 1/2 cup diced onion (75g)
- 1/4 cup ketchup (60g)
- 1 tsp Worcestershire sauce (5ml)
- Salt and pepper to taste
- 2 cups assorted grilled vegetables (carrots, bell peppers, zucchini) (300g)
- 2 cups mashed potatoes (400g)

Instructions:

1. Preheat grill to medium-high heat.
2. In a bowl, mix ground beef, breadcrumbs, milk, egg, diced onion, ketchup, Worcestershire sauce, salt, and pepper. Shape into a loaf.
3. Place meatloaf on a grill-safe baking sheet and grill for 30-35 minutes, until internal temperature reaches 160°F (71°C).
4. Grill assorted vegetables for 4-5 minutes per side until tender.
5. Serve grilled meatloaf with grilled vegetables and mashed potatoes.

Nutritional Facts (Per Serving): Calories: 400 | Sugars: 8g | Fat: 18g | Carbohydrates: 36g | Protein: 26g | Fiber: 6g | Sodium: 400mg

CHAPTER 19: BONUSES

Your Ultimate Guide to Choosing the Perfect Gas Griddle

To make the most of your gas griddle adventures, we've crafted a 30-day grocery shopping guide specifically for our cookbook. This guide streamlines meal preparation by prioritizing fresh, natural ingredients and reducing reliance on processed foods. Pay attention to hidden sugars in sauces and marinades. Adjust quantities as needed, embracing the griddle's ability to enhance the flavors of whole foods. Relish the journey of preparing healthy, delicious meals with your gas griddle! Enjoy the culinary adventure!

Grocery Shopping List for 7-Day Meal Plan

Proteins

Eggs (for Frittata, Steak and Eggs, Breakfast Burrito)
Ground Beef (for Classic Cheeseburger, Mini Meatballs)
Chicken Breast (for Grilled Lemon Herb Chicken, Chicken Alfredo Penne, BBQ Chicken Breast, Buffalo Chicken Sandwich)
Halibut (for Grilled Halibut)
Shrimp (for Grilled Shrimp and Zucchini Boats)
Chorizo (for Burrito)
Bacon (for Quesadilla)
Pulled Pork (for Tacos)
Mahi Mahi (for Grilled Mahi Mahi with Pineapple Salsa)
Baby Back Ribs (for Classic BBQ Baby Back Ribs)

Dairy and Dairy Alternatives:

Shredded Cheese (for Huevos Rancheros, Quesadilla,

Chicken Alfredo Penne, Buffalo Chicken Sandwich)
Parmesan Cheese (for Grilled Asparagus, Spaghetti Carbonara)
Feta Cheese (for Dip Cups)
Butter
Milk or Cream (for Chicken Alfredo Penne, Spaghetti Carbonara)
Greek Yogurt

Fruits:

Pineapple (for Grilled Pineapple, Grilled Mahi Mahi)
Avocado
Mixed Berries (for Fluffy Pancakes with Fresh Berries)
Lemon (for Grilled Lemon Herb Chicken, various recipes)
Mango (for Halibut)
Fig (for Grilled Fig)

Vegetables & Herbs:

Spinach (for Mushroom and Spinach Frittata, Spinach and Artichoke Dip Cups)
Onion (for various recipes)
Red Bell Pepper
Garlic (for various recipes)

Zucchini (for Grilled Shrimp and Zucchini Boats)
Cherry Tomatoes
Asparagus (for Steak and Eggs with Grilled Asparagus, Garlic Parmesan Grilled Asparagus)
Cauliflower (for Grilled Cauliflower Steaks)
Mixed Greens
Fresh Herbs (parsley, cilantro, basil for garnish and flavor)
Mushrooms (for Frittata, various recipes)

Grains & Bakery:

Tortillas (for Huevos Rancheros, Breakfast Quesadilla, BBQ Pulled Pork Breakfast Tacos)
Bread Rolls (for Classic Cheeseburger, Buffalo Chicken Sandwich)
Penne Pasta (for Chicken Alfredo Penne)
Spaghetti (for Spaghetti Carbonara)

Nuts & Seeds:

Pine Nuts
Almonds
Pantry Staples:

Olive Oil (for cooking and dressings)
Honey
Soy Sauce (for Beef Teriyaki Noodles, Chicken Pad Thai)
Balsamic Vinegar (for various dressings)
Salt and Pepper (for seasoning)
Smoked Paprika (for various recipes)
Cumin (for various recipes)
Chili Powder (for various recipes)

Miscellaneous:

Canned Tomatoes (for various recipes)
Tomato Paste (for various recipes)
Chicken Broth (for Chicken Alfredo Penne, various recipes)
Baking Powder (for Fluffy Pancakes)
Vanilla Extract (for Fluffy Pancakes)

Grocery Shopping List for 8-14 Day Meal Plan

Proteins

Eggs (for Protein Pancakes, Grilled Sausage Patties, Ham and Cheese Omelette, Corned Beef Hash)
Chicken Breast (for Pesto Pasta, Grilled Pineapple Chicken, Pesto Chicken Pizza)
Turkey Sausage (for Quesadillas)

Ground Beef (for Philly Cheesesteak Sandwich, BBQ Bacon Burger)
Corned Beef (for Corned Beef Hash)
Sausage Patties (for Grilled Sausage Patties)
Bacon (for BBQ Bacon Burger)
Tilapia (for Herb-Crusted Grilled Tilapia)
Salmon (for Salmon)
Pork Loin (for Pork Loin)
Spare Ribs (for Spare Ribs)
Four Cheese Ravioli (for Four Cheese Ravioli)

Dairy and Dairy Alternatives:

Shredded Cheese (for Turkey Sausage and Spinach Quesadillas, Grilled Sausage Patties, Ham and Cheese Omelette, Baked Ziti)
Parmesan Cheese (for Grilled Zucchini with Parmesan, Baked Ziti)
Cream Cheese (for Tzatziki Sauce, Spinach and Artichoke Dip)
Butter (for Protein Pancakes, Grilled Lemon Bars, various recipes)
Milk or Cream (for Ham and Cheese Omelette, Pesto Chicken Pizza, Baked Ziti)

Fruits:

Pineapple (for Grilled Pineapple Chicken, Grilled Pineapple with Honey and Cinnamon)
Sweet Potatoes (for Sweet Potato and Black Bean Tacos)
Lemons (for Lemon Dill Grilled Salmon, Grilled Lemon Bars)
Bananas (for Chocolate Banana Quesadillas)

Various Fresh Berries (for Protein Pancakes)

Vegetables & Herbs:

Spinach (for Protein Pancakes, Turkey Sausage and Spinach Quesadillas, Spinach and Artichoke Dip)
Onion (for various recipes)
Bell Peppers (for various recipes)
Garlic (for various recipes)
Zucchini (for Grilled Shrimp and Zucchini Boats, Grilled Zucchini with Parmesan)
Corn (for Corn Fritters, Vegetable Fried Rice)
Tomatoes (for Baked Ziti, Grilled Eggplant and Tomato Salad)
Eggplant (for Grilled Eggplant and Tomato Salad)
Fresh Herbs (parsley, cilantro, basil for garnish and flavor)
Cauliflower (for Buffalo Cauliflower Bites)
Jalapeños (for Corn Fritters, Baked Jalapeño Poppers)
Cucumbers (for Tzatziki Sauce)

Grains & Bakery:

Tortillas (for Sweet Potato and Black Bean Tacos, Grilled Veggie Breakfast Tacos)
Bread Rolls (for Philly Cheesesteak Sandwich, BBQ Bacon Burger)
Penne Pasta (for Baked Ziti)
Pizza Dough (for Pesto Chicken Pizza)
Four Cheese Ravioli (for Four Cheese Ravioli)

Nuts & Seeds:

Almond Butter
Pine Nuts

Pantry Staples:

Olive Oil
Honey
Soy Sauce (for Vegetable Fried Rice)
Balsamic Vinegar
Salt and Pepper (for seasoning)
Smoked Paprika
Cumin
Chili Powder (

Miscellaneous:

Canned Tomatoes (for Baked Ziti)
Tomato Paste
Chicken Broth (for Pesto Pasta, Baked Ziti)
Baking Powder (for Protein Pancakes)
Vanilla Extract (for Protein Pancakes)

Grocery Shopping List for 15-21 Day Meal Plan

Proteins:

Eggs (for Huevos Rancheros Tacos, Egg and Sausage Muffins, Beef and Veggie Breakfast Skillet, Mushroom and Spinach Frittata)
Ground Beef (for Spicy Jalapeño Burger, Balsamic Glazed Steak Tips)
Pork Chops (for Maple Glazed Pork Chops)
Sausage (for Egg and Sausage Muffins)

Ribeye Steak (for Grilled Ribeye Steak)
Shrimp (for Shrimp and Avocado Breakfast Tacos, Paella)
Chicken Breast (for Chicken Caesar Wrap, Chicken Alfredo Penne, Chicken Pad Thai)
Tuna Steaks (for Grilled Tuna Steaks with Avocado)
Meatloaf Mix (for Grilled Meatloaf with Veggies)
Swordfish (for Grilled Swordfish with Tomato Basil Relish)

Dairy and Dairy Alternatives:

Shredded Cheese (for Tacos, Muffins, Chicken Caesar Wrap)
Mozzarella Cheese (for Salad)
Ricotta Cheese (for Quesadillas, Crepes)
Cream Cheese (for Spinach and Artichoke Dip Cups)
Butter (for Griddled Chocolate Chip Cookies, various recipes)
Milk or Cream (for Chicken Alfredo Penne, various recipes)

Fruits:

Blueberries (for Blueberry and Ricotta Breakfast Quesadillas, Ricotta and Berry Crepes)
Strawberries (for Grilled Strawberry Shortcake)
Avocados (for Shrimp and Avocado Breakfast Tacos, Grilled Tuna Steaks with Avocado)
Lemons (for various recipes)
Tomatoes (for Grilled Tomato and Mozzarella Salad, various recipes)
Pineapple (for various recipes)

Vegetables & Herbs:

Spinach (for Mushroom and Spinach Frittata, Spinach and Artichoke Dip Cups)
Mushrooms (for Beef and Veggie Breakfast Skillet, Mushroom and Spinach Frittata)
Onion (for various recipes)
Bell Peppers
Jalapeños (for Spicy Jalapeño Burger)
Zucchini (for various recipes)
Fresh Herbs (parsley, cilantro, basil for garnish and flavor)
Mixed Greens
Garlic (for various recipes)

Grains & Bakery:

Tortillas (for Huevos Rancheros Tacos, Shrimp and Avocado Breakfast Tacos)
Bread Rolls (for Spicy Jalapeño Burger)
Penne Pasta (for Chicken Alfredo Penne)
Flour (for Griddled Chocolate Chip Cookies)
Crepe Batter (for Ricotta and Berry Crepes)
Baking Powder
Whole Grain Bread

Nuts & Seeds:

Almonds
Pine Nuts

Pantry Staples:

Olive Oil
Maple Syrup (for Maple Glazed Pork Chops)
Balsamic Vinegar (for Balsamic Glazed Steak Tips)

Soy Sauce (for Chicken Pad Thai)
Honey (for various recipes)
Salt and Pepper (for seasoning)
Smoked Paprika
Cumin (for various recipes)
Chili Powder

Miscellaneous:

Canned Tomatoes
Tomato Paste
Chicken Broth (for Chicken Alfredo Penne, various recipes)
Dark Chocolate (for Griddled Chocolate Chip Cookies)
Cocoa Powder

Grocery Shopping List for 22-28 Day Meal Plan

Proteins:

Eggs (for Burrito, Protein Pancakes, Tacos, Omelette, Steak and Eggs)
Chorizo (for Breakfast Burrito)
Chicken Breast (for Pesto Pasta, BBQ Chicken Breast, Grilled Lemon Herb Chicken)
Ground Beef (for Sandwich, Classic Cheeseburger)
Pork (for BBQ Pulled Pork)
Ribeye Steak
Tilapia
Shrimp (for Grilled Shrimp and Zucchini Boats)
Pork Chops (for Maple Glazed Pork Chops)

Dairy and Dairy Alternatives:

Shredded Cheese (for Breakfast Burrito, Philly

Cheesesteak Sandwich, Four Cheese Ravioli, Ham and Cheese Omelette, Classic Cheeseburger)
Parmesan Cheese (for Spaghetti Carbonara, Garlic Parmesan Grilled Asparagus)
Cream Cheese (for Buffalo Chicken Dip)
Butter (for Protein Pancakes, Garlic Parmesan Grilled Asparagus, Grilled Lemon Bars, various recipes)
Milk or Cream (for Spaghetti Carbonara, Ham and Cheese Omelette, Pesto Pasta)

Fruits:

Avocado (for Breakfast Burrito, various recipes)
Pineapple (for Grilled Pineapple with Honey and Cinnamon)
Lemons (for Herb Chicken, Grilled Lemon Bars)
Berries (for Fluffy Pancakes with Fresh Berries)

Vegetables & Herbs:

Spinach (for various recipes)
Onion (for various recipes)
Bell Peppers
Jalapeños (for Corn Fritters)
Zucchini (for Grilled Zucchini Noodles, Grilled Shrimp and Zucchini Boats)
Asparagus (for Steak, Grilled Asparagus)
Mixed Greens
Tomatoes (for various recipes)
Fresh Herbs (parsley, cilantro, basil for garnish and flavor)
Mushrooms (for Spaghetti Carbonara, various recipes)
Corn (for Corn Fritters)

Grains & Bakery:

Tortillas (for Burrito, Tacos, Grilled Veggie Tacos)
Bread Rolls (for Philly Cheesesteak Sandwich, Classic Cheeseburger)
Ravioli (for Four Cheese Ravioli)
Pasta (for Spaghetti Carbonara, Pesto Pasta)
Flour (for Griddled Chocolate Chip Cookies)
Baking Powder (for Protein Pancakes, various recipes)
Whole Grain Bread

Nuts & Seeds:

Almond Butter (for Protein Pancakes)
Pine Nuts

Pantry Staples:

Olive Oil
Honey
Soy Sauce (for Vegetable Fried Rice)
Balsamic Vinegar
Salt and Pepper (for seasoning)
Smoked Paprika
Cumin
Chili Powder

Miscellaneous:

Canned Tomatoes
Tomato Paste
Chicken Broth (for Pesto Pasta, various recipes)
Dark Chocolate (for Griddled Chocolate Chip Cookies)
Cocoa Powder

Made in the USA
Las Vegas, NV
29 July 2024

93101531R00044